Philosophy and the Event

Philosophy and the Event

Alain Badiou

with Fabien Tarby

Translated by Louise Burchill

polity

First published in French as *La philosophie et l'événement*
© Éditions Germina, 2010

This English edition © Polity Press, 2013
Reprinted in 2014

Polity Press
65 Bridge Street
Cambridge CB2 1UR, UK

Polity Press
350 Main Street
Malden, MA 02148, USA

ISBN-13: 978-0-7456-5394-5 (hardback)
ISBN-13: 978-0-7456-5395-2 (paperback)

A catalogue record for this book is available from the British Library.

Typeset in 11 on 13 pt Sabon
by Toppan Best-set Premedia Limited
Printed and bound in the USA by Edwards Brothers, Inc.

The publisher has used its best endeavours to ensure that the URLs for external websites referred to in this book are correct and active at the time of going to press. However, the publisher has no responsibility for the websites and can make no guarantee that a site will remain live or that the content is or will remain appropriate.

Every effort has been made to trace all copyright holders, but if any have been inadvertently overlooked the publisher will be pleased to include any necessary credits in any subsequent reprint or edition.

For further information on Polity, visit our website: www.politybooks.com

Contents

Translator's Preface

Framing Philosophical Transmission

The interviews that make up this book include a moment of interlocutory self-referentiality in which Alain Badiou points out to Fabien Tarby that the project of transmitting his philosophical ideas by the means of transcribed orally conducted interviews – which is to say by means other than systematic writing – conforms to the founding principle of the entire Platonic edifice: namely, 'the architecture of a philosophical idea exists in itself',[1] such that this has a full autonomy from the textual apparatus that serves habitually as its means of transmission. In difference, then, from works of drama or fiction, philosophy is a protocol of transmission pertaining to something not constituted by the writing process itself. It's for this reason, Badiou insists, that philosophical writing – regardless of its effects of style or literary qualities – is always *didactic* writing: its rationale consists in conveying the Idea and, consequently, in convincing and changing intellectual subjectivities. Yet, it is also the real reason, Badiou adds, for Plato's judging

[1] Cf. infra, pp. 88–9.

writing to be secondary to speech. Speech's superiority
is not – pace Derrida – premised upon a metaphysical
privileging of a full presence that the voice would
supposedly instantiate in an im-mediacy to soul, or
consciousness, but follows from its being a more comprehensive, as well as a more complex, means of *transmission*. Consisting in a 'relation of subjectivity to the
Idea' that cannot be reduced to a form of knowledge
alone, philosophy requires for its complete, and not
exclusively intellectual or discursive, transmission a
transference onto the person of the philosopher – in
other words, an amorous receptivity or, as Badiou puts
it slightly differently elsewhere, 'the encounter with a
master'[2] – which is precisely what the scene of speech
sets the frame for: the corporeal presence of the philosopher, the resonance of his or her voice are the essential
'props', so to speak, for the full staging of the Idea and,
accordingly, the latter's orchestration of subjectivity.
Certainly, there is still a value given to 'presence' within
this philosophical scene yet, in view of the latter's functioning as a veritable 'machine of subjectivization', this
value is in no way simple, immediate or transparent:
'the body of the other [the philosopher] has to be there,
his or her voice has to resound',[3] but these are both
variables within a shifting set of relations that act to
ensure the circulation, crafting and capture of affects
and forces no less than elements of knowledge or
thought.

Whatever Badiou's insistence on the transference
effects that accompany spoken discourse, however, his
comparison of speech and writing aims, above all,
at showing that the rationalist imperative of transmission transcends each and every mode it may take. 'The
transmission of thought is indifferent to language' is a

---

[2] Badiou, Alain, 'L'Aveu du philosophe', in Marianne Alphant (ed.),
La Vocation philosophique, Paris: Bayard, 2004, p. 149.
[3] Cf. infra, p. 54.

formulation, found elsewhere in his work,[4] that makes the same point, all while more boldly situating ideas' autonomy in respect not simply to language's written or spoken forms but to its substantive individuations as such. No national language, such as English or French, would impress, in other words, a singularity on the concepts it conveys; with Badiou not hesitating in this way to resurrect something of the order of transcendent signifieds – again, as it were, pace Derrida. Yet, while his dismissal of any linguistic condition bearing upon the transmission of thought is undoubtedly directed primarily to 'sophistic' thinkers who would accredit language with 'carving out' everything that has been envisaged as 'being',[5] it comports no less emphatically a great number of consequences for those equally, if otherwise, concerned with language's crafting of concepts: namely, translators. Pre-eminent amongst these is that no term of a national language can legitimately be considered 'untranslatable' – other than in the sense, at least, that, insofar as certain words or certain semantic constellations highlight particularly acutely the differences between one language and another, their translation can never be considered as 'assured'.[6] Entailing a diagnosis of contrasting linguistic and cultural realities at a given moment in time, the translation of such 'untranslatables' is not only never a matter of 'superimposition' but an act invariably calling for constantly reiterated probation.

One such word of the French language p d particular problems in translating these interview nto English.

---

[4] Badiou, Alain, 'Français: De la langue française comme évidement', in Cassin, Barbara (ed.), *Vocabulaire européen des philosophies*, Paris: Editions du Seuil/Dictionnaires Le Robert, 2004, p. 466.
[5] Cf. infra, p. 113.
[6] See Cassin, Barbara, 'Présentation' in *Vocabulaire européen des philosophies*, Paris: Editions du Seuil/Dictionnaires Le Robert, 2004, pp. xvii–xviii.

The term involved – *dispositif* – is not, it must be stated from the start, one of Badiou's philosophical concepts. Unlike 'event', 'void', 'multiple' or 'truth', or again, say, 'forcing' or 'compatibility', *dispositif* plays no crucial, intrinsic role in the articulation of Badiou's system of thought and is, as such, neither defined nor in any sense 're-marked' by Badiou on the occasions he employs it. It would seem, simply, a word of the French language at his (thought's) disposal. Yet, as any reader of contemporary French theory is well aware, *dispositif* is far from being 'just' a lexical item in Badiou's national language. It has the status of an important concept in the work of Michel Foucault from the mid 1970s on, and has given rise, on this basis, to texts by both Gilles Deleuze and Giorgio Agamben (amongst others) set on explicating its meaning. Its emergence as a concept predates, nonetheless, Foucault's use, being seemingly first endowed with a precise theoretical sense in two seminal texts written on cinema by Jean-Louis Baudry in 1970 and 1975 respectively.[7] Since the late 1970s, moreover, *dispositif* proliferates as both an analytical concept and a technical term in just about every theoretical or operational field in France one can think of: from media and communications to psychoanalysis, traffic flow management to the analysis of funeral rites, education to . . . translation studies.[8] In most of these cases – to cite from

---

[7] Baudry, Jean-Louis, [1970] 'Ideological Effects of the Basic Cinematographic Apparatus' and [1975] 'The Apparatus: Metapsychological Approaches to the Impression of Reality in the Cinema', in L. Braudy and M. Cohen (eds), *Film Theory and Criticism: Introductory Readings*, New York: Oxford University Press, 2004, pp. 206–23 & 355–65. While Baudry doesn't define the concept of *dispositif* in the first of these two articles, he does use the term there in the sense that he attributes to it as a key concept five years later.
[8] See Kessler, Frank, 'Notes on *dispositif*' (May 2006), http://www.let.uu.nl/~Frank.Kessler/personal/notes on dispositif.PDF; and Ladmiral, Jean René 'Pour une philosophie de la traduction', *Revue de Métaphysique et de Morale*, n° 1, 1989, pp. 5–22.

the 1999 issue of a French social science journal entirely dedicated to exploring the use and propagation of the concept – *dispositif* refers to 'a configuration of heterogeneous elements' that is 'arranged in such a way that it affords the optimal conditions for the implementation of certain actions or certain events'.[9] Or again, as another, more recent, source dealing with the term's broad diffusion over the last 40 years puts it, 'a *dispositif* is taken to be a material [. . . or] in some cases even a conceptual or strategic framework making it possible for a given type of phenomenon to occur.'[10] In short, as established in the French language since the mid to late 1970s, *dispositif*'s broad sense – which also furnishes, in fact, the general contour of its conceptual deployment by Baudry and Foucault – would seem to be that of 'a multiform something set up in a certain way for a certain end'.

While *dispositif* is not a concept in Badiou's system of thought, the fact that it is in the work of Foucault, Baudry, Deleuze and Agamben, has, of course, generated what are by now standard ways of translating the term as used by these authors, with these renderings having increasingly become, in turn, the norm for occurrences of *dispositif* in basically any theoretical text at all. Leaving aside, therefore, the precise definitions Foucault, Baudry, Deleuze and Agamben give to the term, let's simply note that, as used by these, amongst other, authors, *dispositif* is either translated into English as 'apparatus' or not, in fact, translated at all; the French term being erected in the latter case into a ('true') 'untranslatable' that can only function as a form of 'referential marker' in the English texts within which it circulates. The English titles of Deleuze's and Agamben's respective texts exploring the concept as fashioned by

---

[9] Vandendorp, Florence, 'Un cadre plus que normative: Les pratiques funéraires', *Hermès*, n° 25, 1999.
[10] Kessler, op. cit.

Foucault are in this respect paradigmatic: namely, 'What is a *dispositif*?', in the first instance, and 'What is an Apparatus?', in the second – even if Agamben was himself to propose the far less standard 'What is a Dispositor?'[11] That the only alternative to non-translation would, though, indeed seem 'apparatus' is brought out even more eloquently by Baudry's use of the term equally being rendered this way, despite the cinema theorist expressly distinguishing *dispositif* from *appareil* – a French word that, for reasons of tradition as much as those of semantics, has itself to be rendered as . . . 'apparatus'. While a conceptual distinction between 'apparatus' and 'apparatus' would hardly seem enlightening for readers of Baudry in English, there are, of course, reasons for choosing to render *dispositif* in such a way. Of the definitions given for *dispositif* in French language dictionaries, the sense that is qualified as 'technical' or 'technological' is, indeed, that of *appareil*, which, as just seen, is standardly translated as 'apparatus' – even if this synonym is absent from bilingual French–English dictionaries' definition for *dispositif*'s technical sense, where one finds, instead, the more concrete 'appliance', 'mechanism' or 'device'. Since both Foucault's and Baudry's use of *dispositif* in no way refers to a mechanical device but – put broadly – a network or structure comprised of heterogeneous elements that gives rise to certain effects of subjectivization, it's easy to understand the translators' choice of 'apparatus', which, other than its technical definition of

---

[11] Agamben proposed this translation in a lecture given in 2005. See 'What is a Dispositor?', lecture transcript by Jason Michael Adams, http://www.16beavergroup.org/mtarchive/archives/002884print. html. See also Agamben, Giorgio, *'What Is an Apparatus?' and Other Essays*, trans. David Kishik and Stefan Pedatella, Stanford: Standford University Press, 2009, and Deleuze, Gilles, 'What is a *dispositif*?', in *Michel Foucault, Philosopher*, trans. Timothy J. Armstrong, New York and London: Routledge, 1992, pp. 159–68.

'appliance', also has a meaning close to 'system', as in 'police apparatus', 'party apparatus', and so on. And indeed, on the level of their general linguistic and semantic construction, Foucault's various apparatuses – 'apparatus of power', 'apparatus of the prison', 'apparatus of sexuality' – do work well overall in English. As for 'the set of perceptual, psychological, physiological, social as well as technical mechanisms involved in a film's screening/viewing situation' that is Baudry's *dispositif*, this calls for retranslation.

That admitted, the reasons adduced for not translating *dispositif* are of more immediate interest here insofar as, on at least one occasion in his work when Badiou does, in fact, use *dispositif* in a systematic manner – in his text 'Being, Existence, Thought: Prose and Concept' – the translator's choice is to retain the French.[12] On the whole, the basis for judging there to be 'no suitable English equivalent' for *dispositif* has to do with the extension or polysemy of the French term, which is usually accorded four definitions: in a strictly juridical sense, it refers to the part of a judgement that contains the decision separate from the opinion, or to the enacting clause of a law; in a military context, it refers to the manner in which forces and equipment are arranged and deployed in conformity with a plan – e.g., *dispositif d'attaque*, 'plan of attack' or *dispositif de défense*, 'defence system'; its third sense is the technical one of 'apparatus' or 'device' noted above, but also the 'arrangement of the pieces making up such a mechanical device'; while the fourth, noted as 'figurative', is glossed

---

[12] See Badiou, Alain, *Handbook of Inaesthetics*, Stanford: Stanford University Press, 2005. The translator of this text, Alberto Toscano, refers to the reasons given by Daniel W. Smith, in a note to his translation of Deleuze's 'Desire and Pleasure', for leaving *dispositif* in the French. These come down to the lack of 'a suitable English equivalent', with Smith furnishing a list of *dispositif*'s diverse definitions as argumentation.

by a series of synonyms, such as 'arrangement', 'method' or 'procedure': this being the sense, referred to earlier, having known an all-pervasive proliferation over the last forty years.[13] In this light, the unsuitability of 'apparatus' as a strict equivalent of *dispositif* is obvious: the word's mechanical connotations remain too accentuated while it fails to convey the overarching meaning of 'arrangement' that is found in all of the French term's different definitions in conformity with *dispositif*'s derivation from the verb *disposer*, 'to arrange', 'to lay out', 'to range'. The underlying problem here is, however, not one peculiar to *dispositif* alone; it being a matter, quite to the contrary, of an intrinsic difference between French and English that has been described in terms of an opposition between these languages' 'level of abstraction' and 'level of the real'.[14] Put succinctly, French is a language that functions at a higher level of abstraction than does English, such that it is completely commonplace for a French word to serve as a common denominator, as it were, for a whole series of synonyms in English that are unable to be grouped under a generic or 'umbrella' term in the latter language itself. One very 'down-to-earth' example is the concept of *promenade*, for which English can but offer a profusion of designations for its particular instances: thus, 'walk', 'stroll' or 'hike' for *promenade à pied*, 'drive' or 'ride' for *promenade en voiture*, (bike-)'ride' for *promenade en vélo*, 'sail' for *promenade en bateau*, and so on.[15] That said, what's interesting in the case of *dispositif* is that the English words that could be proposed for the French

---

[13] I've consulted here the 1978 edition of *Le Robert*, which is, therefore, roughly contemporary with the English translations – all first published between 1974 and 1978 – of the texts by Foucault and Baudry in which *dispositif* was to emerge as a concept.

[14] Vinay, J.-P. and Darbelnet, J. *Stylistique comparé du français et de l'anglais*, Paris: Didier, 1977, pp. 58–62.

[15] Ibid., p. 59.

term as used generically – such as 'apparatus' or 'arrangement', 'set-up' or 'structure'[16] – would seem either, indeed too concrete or too much on the 'level of the real' ('apparatus', 'set-up'), or, almost paradoxically, not specific enough ('arrangement', 'structure') by dint of their lacking something of the term's 'constructivist', strategic or functional aspect. In short, what English seems to lack as a suitable equivalent for *dispositif* is a word capable of conveying the concept of a generic structure or arrangement which would at the same time be characterized by a specific kind of 'constructivism' of its relations and elements.

Now, just as Badiou's use of *dispositif* in his interviews with Tarby is in no way a systematic conceptual deployment, nor is it generic. The occasions on which he uses the term are all contextually specific and, as such, qualified: the *dispositifs* of which he speaks are 'mathematical' or 'physical', 'rational' or 'formal', or, indeed, 'transcendent' (in reference to a particular philosophical position), without these being understood as variants of a precisely defined type of formation. It makes no sense, in other words, to ask in Badiou's case, unlike that of Baudry, Foucault, Deleuze or Agamben: 'what is (his understanding of) a *'dispositif'*?' This being the case, not to translate the occurrences of *dispositif* in these interviews would have amounted not only to according the term, as 'untranslatable', a quasi-sacrosanct, or even transcendent, status, but, equally, to endowing it with an unwarranted conceptual signification. Such a 'conceptual reification' is, that said, an ever-present risk or danger in translating philosophy, being fuelled as it is by the apprehension of obscuring

---

[16] That said, 'structure' is inappropriate as a translation for *dispositif* since it is precisely the attempt to circumvent the wholistic, static and, in a sense, transcendent connotations attributed to *structure* that motivated the emergence of *dispositif* within a 'poststructuralist' paradigm in the seventies.

within the folds of another language the traces of something that might prove essential to the archaeology of a philosopher's work or thought. So it is that, despite Badiou's use of *dispositif* in these interviews being 'obviously' indebted to the latter's discursive proliferation since the late 1970s, one can still, even after having decided not to retain the French, hesitate to translate it in different ways in accordance with context and the constellation of English synonyms covered by the French term. After all, given its conceptual status in Foucault, Deleuze and Agamben, might there not be a subterranean irrigation of its occurrences in Badiou's remarks that needs to be respected? Or, more simply, given that its translation is so often purported impossible in virtue of a conceptual – or even purely, lexical – singularity of the French, shouldn't its passage into English be at the very least uniformly marked and manifestly flagged? There is, in this sort of apprehension, something akin perhaps – in thinking back to Badiou's remarks concerning the philosophical scene of speech – to a transference effect, whose object, if not simply the 'master's word', would be a certain figure, at least, of 'the concept' – be this, in fact, an assured figure or not. Whence the pre-eminent concern, as in any transference, with the integrity of the object: the signifier's presence – as Derrida, again, might have put it – is, above all, to be kept intact so as to avoid fragmenting, or disguising by dissemination, that which might reveal itself to have an unsuspected potency. Of course, in the case of a thinker's concepts, this type of concern for the signifier's integrity and terminological consistency is absolutely essential, but when it extends to 'commonplace' words, however conceptually reworked by others, or, say, terms that are simply commonly used by the author – *déploiement* is, for example, one such word in Badiou's vocabulary that is often uniformly rendered by its English cognate 'deployment' even when other equivalents, such as 'implementation' or 'application', better suit the context

– this apprehension of losing something of the French original's unique semantic network should surely be tempered. After all, all words, in any language, have singular semantic networks that are impossible to super-impose in their entirety with regard to other languages. Were one to aim at an absolute fidelity to the letter of the text, one would, in fact, not translate at all.

This brings us back to the *dispositif* of Badiou's and Tarby's interviews – in the sense here both of the word's occurrences in Badiou's remarks and the discursive 'format' or 'scene of speech' that served as the frame-work in which these were made. It will be remembered that Badiou refers to the interview situation as confirm-ing Plato's principle of philosophy's autonomy from the textual apparatus that serves as its means of transmis-sion. Interestingly, something of this autonomy seemed equally confirmed in the act of these interviews' transla-tion, to the extent, at least, that translating Badiou's speech rather than his systematic writing proved to qualify or put into perspective the apprehension of fore-going something of a word's singular semantic constel-lation. The reason for this has to do, principally, with speech's far greater informality and linearity: over the course of these interviews, Badiou is often led, for example, to proffer a rapid succession of different ways of formulating or designating the same basic 'signified' or semantic notion that he is concerned with conveying; had his thoughts been systematically written down, on the other hand, and, thus, subject to revision and re-structuration, such a cluster of synonyms or alternative expressions would undoubtedly be replaced by a more punctual designation, both more abstract and more 'enshrined', so to speak, by the syntax. In translating speech, as a result, the apprehension of losing some-thing *essential* to a word's semantic network is often counteracted by the very context: a slew of French syn-onyms being presented, say, for *déploiement*, the trans-lator is not only summoned to use a variety of English equivalents but reassured that these can serve in other circumstances – including systematic texts – where *déploiement* is used alone. Context is, of course, of paramount importance in a broader sense as well. Badiou's use of *dispositif* in a discussion with Tarby on quantum physics is hardly likely to harbour a reference to Foucault's, Deleuze's or Agamben's conceptual definition, or, for that matter, to have an undetermined, generic extension. Were he to be speaking about a *dispositif expérimental*, this could be an 'experimental set-up' or, indeed, an 'experimental apparatus', in English – but most definitely not an 'experimental *dispositif*.' Given, though, that Badiou's reference in these interviews is, in fact, to quantum physics' conceptual framework, his opposition of a *dispositif mathématique* and a *dispositif physique* would seem best rendered, accordingly, as one between a mathematical and a physical 'framework'.[17]

As indicated, I've chosen to translate the eight occurrences of *dispositif* in these interviews as 'set-up' when the sense is relatively concrete or technical, and as 'framework' in instances where Badiou is referring to more abstract structures. There are, of course, specific reasons I could adduce for these choices – other than those, that is, that this preface has so far outlined in terms of the necessity of capturing, as far as possible and according to context, both *dispositif*'s constructivist sense and the term's overarching definition of 'an arrangement enabling the implementation of certain actions or certain events'. 'Framework', in particular, intersects with *dispositif* in the translation of philosophy in that both terms have been proposed, along with 'enframing' (and, for that matter, 'setting-up'), for the German word *Ge-stell*, which, while meaning in ordinary usage an apparatus (*Gerät*), is employed by Heidegger to designate a key concept in his reflection

[17] See infra., p. 99.

on technology. While an etymological similarity exists
between the French and German terms – as well, again,
as with the English 'set-up' ('to set', like the German
stellen, corresponds to the Latin *ponere*, such that 'set-
up' and *Ge-stell* intersect with *dis-positio, dis-ponere*)[18]
– the choice of 'framework' as a rendering of Heidegger's concept rests largely on a proximity of register
and semantic extension. This is not to say, however, that
'framework' corresponds to *Ge-stell* in all circumstances
. . . any more than it does to all occurrences of *dispositif*.
And inversely, the lack of a *strict* equivalent in English
for *dispositif* in its generic sense entails neither ceasing
to probe English for a suitable conceptual synonym, nor
forgoing the use of words capable of capturing the
term's meaning in other circumstances. Some such
words are 'scene' when used in English phrases such as
'scene of speech', 'machine' as in 'machine of subjectivization', 'apparatus' as in 'textual apparatus', or 'situation' as in 'interview situation'; with all the English
phrases just cited being translations of, or translatable
by, French locutions with *dispositif*. We return in this
way, as concerns philosophical translation at least,
to the principle that, for Badiou, would find a confirmation in these very interviews: thought being primary,
the means by which this is framed – speech, writing
or, indeed, language per se – are subservient to its
transmission.

Louise Burchill

---

[18] See Agamben, Giorgio, '*What Is an Apparatus?*', op.cit., p. 12;
and Borgman, Albert, with Mitcham, Carl, 'The Question of
Heidegger and Technology: A Critical Review of the Literature',
Philosophy Today, vol. 31, no. 2/4, Summer 1987, p. 109.

Acknowledgements

I would like to thank, above all, Jennifer McCamley, who meticulously inspected drafts of sections of this translation, and Catherine Perrel and Marie-Cécile Fauvin for offering guidance with particularly intricate, syntactic constructions in Badiou's French. Alain Badiou, Fabien Tarby, Isabelle Vodoz, Justin Clemens and Eon Yorck provided much appreciated assistance with points of persistent interrogation, while Sarah Lambert and Susan Beer at Polity Press respectively steered and finely tuned the translation process as a whole.

My profound gratitude goes, equally, to the European Translation Centre for Literature and Human Sciences, EKEMEL – now, alas, a victim of the calamitous policies applied to Greece – and the Municipality of Paros for granting me a translator's residency at the *Spiti Logotechnias* (House of Literature) at Lefkes village, Paros, in order to work on this book. It is to the inhabitants of Paros who have fought to ensure that the *Spiti Logotechnias* remains a centre for the art, or craft, of 'logoi' that my final thanks are due.

Foreword

I think back to the hours of dialogue that now make up these pages. Alain Badiou embraced the project of a book of interviews on his work with simplicity and a keen attention. They were moments of great intellectual and human intensity.

The idea of setting five themes very quickly imposed itself: what better trajectory could there be than one traversing the four conditions of politics, love, art and science, to end up with philosophy?

Taking politics as the theme for the first interview turned out to be a particularly happy choice. It proved to be a first level of entry to the work and made it possible to define, in a context immediately comprehensible to everyone, philosophical notions that would, doubtlessly, have been more difficult to broach directly. It was a fairly logical next step to then go on to the interviews on love, which was equally the case for the interviews that followed on art, science and philosophy. This means that the dialogue in, and of, itself became, in the most fitting manner, an introduction to the thought. The warmth and enthusiasm that Alain Badiou brought to this project are largely responsible for this.

Readers will find at the end of the book my 'Short Introduction to Alain Badiou's Philosophy'. It is a complement, a supplement, and a new occasion to traverse the work.

I encourage, then, readers who are seeking an initiation to this momentous philosophy to plunge into the text, leaving to one side whatever qualms they may have concerning its difficulty. They will inevitably find themselves carried to the core of Alain Badiou's thought by the very movement of these interviews. The philosopher himself will guide them.

All things considered, have we here a book that satisfies the wish of the editor, Jean Tellez, for a 'general introduction to Alain Badiou's philosophy'? It is up to the reader to judge. I hope so, in any case. I must, that said, state what this experience has been for me: namely, a revitalized view of this philosophy, astonishing rediscoveries, and a direct and enthusiastic encounter with a work that I've been reading and reflecting on for years. I would like to express my profound gratitude to Alain Badiou.

Isabelle Vodoz helped, in her usual attentive and rigorous manner, with the elaboration of this book. I am sincerely grateful to her as well.

Fabien Tarby

1

Politics

The political field today: the Left/Right opposition and consensus

– Alain Badiou, politics has an essential place in your life and work. You view it, moreover, as one of what you call philosophy's *conditions*. It is, then, a good place for us to begin tackling your philosophy. First, hasn't it become difficult today to be involved in politics? I'd also like to hear how you define it. What is politics, the truth of politics?

– We really have to take into account the system of constraints in which people find themselves today. What is their margin of manoeuvre? What freedom do they have? For there to be true politics, the framework within which things take place has to be both clear and held in common. For example, if society is a society of classes with conflicting interests, then politics will lie within this framework. If the established order rests upon a collective organization totally at odds with equality, politics will have to deal, locally and globally, with this issue. Politics always has to do with what one knows, and experiences, regarding the nature of contradictions. I think that in the great political tradition we've inherited – a heritage that, moreover, disconcerts us and puts us ill at ease – the fundamental point is that there are enemies. There are not just adversaries, but enemies. There are people whose worldview and what they inflict upon, and expect of, us is something we deem completely unacceptable.

Bringing the notion of the enemy into focus like this has always been the perspective of the great tradition of politics, particularly its revolutionary tradition – with 'revolutionary' understood in a fairly vague sense, extending from the French Revolution up to the 1980s. The problem is that this notion is absolutely confused today. This is the case for two reasons. First, on a worldwide scale, the collapse of the Soviet Union put an end to a duality that had furnished a very clear, objective framework: there were two camps, two orientations, two models. Then, on an intra-State level, the facts of class have been erased in favour of the idea that our societies are ones in which there is an uninterrupted expansion of the middle class. The prevailing idea everywhere is that the middle class is the veritable basis of democratic politics: an immense middle class that pushes to its margins, on the one side, a small kernel of the very rich who, while unfortunately 'inevitable', are nevertheless very few, and, on the other side, a small number of very poor and very exploited people. This is the idea, presented as a consensual one, that there are debates, discussions and divergences, but not enemies in the strict sense.

– Would you say that the main problem today is less an absence of political consciousness than a difficulty or refusal to become involved, a loss of militant spirit?

– I'd say that the difficulty today is to extricate oneself from consensus. This is a real difficulty. It's not enough to want to escape from it, to decide you are going to escape from it. It's much more complicated than that. You are faced with a constitutive given of our societies. Our societies no longer really recognize any enemies except external ones, such as Al Qaeda, Islamic terrorism and so on. We've gone back to the idea that the main contradiction is between the civilized and the barbarians. But when the main contradiction is between the civilized and the barbarians, as at the time of the fall of the Roman Empire, politics no longer exists. There is the police, there is possibly war, but there isn't politics. We have to rid ourselves of the idea that the main contradiction is that between civilized and barbarians. We have to escape, as a result, from consensus. This maintains that everyone agrees, minor reservations aside, with the evaluation that society is not going to change. Capitalism in the economy and parliamentary democracy in politics is, basically, a really good combination – that's what consensus maintains. The crisis made this particularly clear: everyone agreed on saving the ship and, in particular, on saving the banks, even though these were directly responsible for the financial seism.

Under these conditions, it is hard to be involved or to be militant because this requires you to have a minimal sense of rupture or a non-consensual state of mind. You have to have the conviction that something needs to be done that escapes the law of the world. This difficulty of becoming involved is also linked to the difficulty of knowing from where you would start from today in order to criticize the prevailing state of things, how this would get off the ground and how it would be organized. The general frameworks that held previously aren't valid any more. You can't refer any longer to the battle between the imperialist and socialist camps or, in any clear way, to the contradiction between the bourgeoisie and the proletariat. You can't have the slightest confidence any more in the last remaining soft contradiction, namely that between the Left and the Right.

When all is said and done, where is the enemy? Where is the friend? These questions have become extraordinarily confused. If you're pessimistic, you'll conclude that we are in a period in which politics, strictly speaking, has purely and simply disappeared. It's not because there are debates about the State or the economy that there is politics. Politics is a strong subjective activity, capable of producing new truths. Can it, in this sense, survive under the present conditions? This is an open question. Under the reign of Louis XIV, there was no, or very little, politics, just like at the end of the Roman Empire. There are, then, historical sequences practically empty of politics. The difficulty of which you speak is, as a result, crucial; it bears on the possibility, or the real, of politics today.

– Would you say, similarly, that being on the Left maintains a relation to truth whereas taking up a position on the Right has strictly no meaning other than a structural one, where it's a matter of seeking satisfaction in the world as it is, in the sense of everyone's animal appetites being satisfied: the acceptance of the real, in short?

– If you say that, you're taking 'Left' in a different sense from the one prevailing today, where to be on the Left means taking up a certain place within the prevailing political system called 'democracy'. Left and Right are integral givens of all the great democracies that, succinctly put, are qualified as 'Western'. You're on the Left when – everything else being, in other respects, the same – you propose to distribute a little bit more of the existing profit to the disinherited social strata. I don't see anything else in the Left today. In this sense, it is simply a category forming part of the consensus – a category that the system absolutely needs. The system vitally depends on a falsified contradiction, on a game consisting in fictitiously designating enemies on the basis of subtle differences, which are, in fact, what drives the game of pseudo-politics. But I fully see that you take 'Left' in a different sense.

– Yes, not the 'Left' in a structural sense but in what might be called an 'evental' one. In the structural sense, the Left is taken up in the system of consensus you're talking about and which it, ultimately, doesn't question either politically or even economically. Whereas the Left in an evental sense never relinquishes the notion of a veritable rupture taking place. This is its goal. And it's in these terms that you think of the political event: something has to happen that changes what's given, changes the structure.

– I don't know if the word 'Left' can be held onto in this case. If it is, then 'Left' will indeed refer to a politics that both aims and works at bringing out the truth of the collectivity, the truth of what this is really capable of in terms of creation, innovation and even values. Politics is, then, all the processes by means of which human collectivity becomes active or proves capable of new possibilities as regards its own destiny. In this case, I accept your definition. The Left is the process of a truth, the Right merely the management of things, of what there is. This is why, moreover, as is the case in almost all representative democracies, the Right is usually in power: it is homogeneous with what there is. The Left comes to power from time to time when somewhat unusual problems crop up which the Right finds hard to resolve.

I will define, then, the parliamentary Left as an adjustment variable of the system as a whole. It's possible to show that it comes to power in periods when public opinion has to be readjusted to capitalism. One of the tasks of Mitterrand's presidency was precisely to set into motion financial liberalization, which was very largely carried out while Bérégovoy was prime minister.[1] This liberalization was necessary to adjust opinion to the variables of contemporary global capitalism. It wasn't the Right that carried out this adjustment but the Left; the Right simply continued the movement. Blair, for his part, pursued the path that Thatcher had brutally opened up. When my English friends say that Blair was 'Thatcher with a human face', their definition is spot on.

– You show a mistrust, or an incredulity perhaps, towards organizations placed on the far Left or qualified as 'radical Left'. I'm thinking in particular of your positions concerning the *Nouveau Parti Anticapitaliste*.[2] Yet isn't their strategy compatible with yours? Can't one fight the system from inside and at the same time appeal to the event? The logic of the NPA isn't necessarily contradictory to yours, while, on the other hand, yours seems to be contradictory to theirs.

– I'd like to say, first of all, that it's not up to the philosopher to define a political strategy. What interests me is philosophy's being consistently positioned with regard to political innovation and not to politics' old or

---

[1] Pierre Bérégovoy served as prime minister under François Mitterrand from 1992 to 1993. [Translator's note]

[2] *Nouveau Parti Anticapitaliste*: The New Anticapitalist Party was founded in 2009, after the dissolution of the Revolutionary Communist League (*Ligue Communiste Révolutionnaire*, LCR), which was the strongest far Left party in France at that time. Unlike the LCR, the NPA does not claim a specific relation to Trotskyism but heralds itself as a pluralistic and democratic party, aiming to unify the fractured movements of the French radical Left and attract new activists. Its 'founding principles' set out the need to overthrow existing institutions and call for 'social revolution' but do not refer to any particular revolutionary theory. [Translator's note]

repetitive forms, of which the NPA is a very particular example. My problem is that I can barely see any difference between what the NPA does and what the Communist Party at the height of its glory did: namely, combine two flanks in an ordered and systematic way. On the one side, we find an intra-parliamentary activity, consisting of standing for elections, vying for the greatest possible number of votes and refusing compromising alliances. On the other side, there are social struggles, in which the party participates actively, with non-negligible attempts at infiltrating union bureaucracies. The Communist Party carried all this out to perfection. It had an electoral force of enormous amplitude, up to 20 to 25 per cent in its best periods. Moreover, it had hold over the main union, the CGT.[3] It combined a hefty presence in workers' and popular struggles with the conquest of electoral bastions, mainly municipal ones like the 'red banlieues'.[4] The NPA hasn't created anything new in respect to this. Ultimately, the NPA is the typical far Left, with one eye on the State and elections and the other on 'civil society' and social struggles. The philosopher doesn't judge this kind of initiative with militant categories of the type 'you're right-wing' or 'you're betraying the revolution'. He simply notes that it's a matter of repetition and that whatsoever has the force of a political condition of philosophy cannot be of the order of repetition.

[3] The CGT or *Confédération générale du travail* (General Confederation of Labour) is the largest of the five major French confederations of trade unions. It was dominated by the French Communist Party (PCF) from 1947 until the 1990s, when it cut all organic links with the latter. [Translator's note]
[4] The *banlieues rouges* ('red banlieues') are the outskirt districts of Paris where, traditionally, the French Communist Party held mayorships and other elected positions. [Translator's note]

Media and propaganda

– The NPA, in your view, is then barking up the wrong tree because it believes that it's possible for an event to come about within the framework of consensual democracy. The media system makes up a large part of this framework. How do you see this system as functioning?

– I think that the ruling apparatus and the power of the State have always, historically, made use of extremely powerful propaganda apparatuses. I often give an example that I find striking. Sure, people are in front of their TV night after night. But in France, before the eighteenth century, even the tiniest village had a church with its priest – an immense building that ruled over the daily routines of ordinary people, the chiming of its bells regulating everyday life. The priest would hear confessions and take the pulpit every Sunday to declare what people had to do and think. It was an absolutely remarkable propaganda apparatus, glorifying the King before a congregation of the faithful who were, for the most part, illiterate. It was the only structured speech people heard. Today, we've forgotten all that. The churches are deserted. In the villages, they are nothing more than monuments in a state of semi-ruin. Yet, when all that was living, it constituted an unbelievably wide-ranging and powerful propaganda apparatus that both structured people's lives internally and organized the transmission of traditions. Today, with the media, we have a technological, differentiated apparatus. Are we to consider that this has a greater, more obvious influence than the propaganda apparatus I've just mentioned? This is not at all evident. The present-day propaganda apparatus is like society as a whole. On one hand, it is the organ of consensus – and all the more so given that it's in the hands of the great financial powers. On the other, it is probably more diversified and less crudely ideological than the archaic propaganda of the Church or monarchistic State was. Sure, it organizes opinion just as all mass propaganda does. Yet, in parliamentary democratic countries, opinion is summoned to obey only very broadly, not in detail. Today's propaganda, as indubitable, massive and dominant as it is in my eyes, leaves a fair amount of slack on the level of individual behaviours, whereas the previous forms of propaganda left very little.

The true nature of the media system seems to me to lie in consensus itself, in the sense that it's because consensus rules that the media is what they are. I don't think that the media construct consensus. Rather, it's consensus that makes people put up with the media's repetitive mediocrity and paucity of information. People thrive on this moreover, they revel in it; they chip in their contribution and go play their part. You have to see the way the media summon people and how people adore this. They are thrilled to go and announce that they are part of the process. They're ready to do all it takes to keep the media show going. Basically, the media are to opinion what elections are to the State: a voluntary indoctrination.

The event

– We've just spoken about the structures of our time. You oppose to these the possibility of the event. What, though, is, in fact, a political event?

– For me, an event is something that brings to light a possibility that was invisible or even unthinkable. An event is not by itself the creation of a reality; it is the creation of a possibility, it opens up a possibility. It indicates to us that a possibility exists that has been ignored. The event is, in a certain way, merely a proposition. It proposes something to us. Everything will depend on the way in which the possibility proposed by the event is grasped, elaborated, incorporated and set out in the world. This is what I name a 'truth procedure'. The event creates a possibility but there, then, has to be an effort – a group effort in the political context, an individual one in the case of artistic creation – for this possibility to become real; that is, for it to be inscribed, step by step, in the world. It's a matter, here, of the consequences in the real world of the rupture that the event is. I speak of truth because something is created that sets down, not simply the law of the world, but its truth.

Events are the creation in the world of the possibility of a truth procedure and not that which create this procedure itself. Examples can be given in all domains, extra-political as well as political ones. The simplest example is love. It's said that you 'fall in love'. You meet someone. It so happens that between you and he or she, between he or she and you, an unexpected and unforeseeable possibility opens up in your personal, empirical existence. This doesn't mean that love is formed by the encounter on its own. It will be necessary to live something; there will have to be consequences. The encounter is the opening in my own life of a possibility that wasn't calculable in advance. A political event, like the assault on the Tuileries palace in 1792 or like March 1871, when one tried to take the Parisians' canons away from them – an incident which sparked off the Paris Commune – is, similarly, the apparition of a possibility (the Republic, workers' power . . .) that was previously unperceived. A political event today, whatever its scale, is a local opening up of political possibilities.

– But there is always, of course, a dominant structure that is opposed to the event and to what this proffers of an unprecedented nature: that the impossible become possible.

– Yes, and that's precisely what power, the State, the state of things, is; it's what claims to have the monopoly of possibilities. It's not simply what governs the real. It's what pronounces that which is possible and impossible. This is very important as regards the contemporary period. The power in place doesn't ask us to be convinced that it does everything very well – moreover, there is always an opposition to say that it does everything very badly – but to be convinced that it's the only thing possible. With a political event, a possibility emerges that escapes the prevailing power's control over possibles. All of a sudden people, sometimes masses of people, start to think there is another possibility. They gather together to discuss it, they form new organizations. They may make some immense errors but that's not the important point. They make the possibility opened up by the event come alive.

I think that this is the way things happen in all types of creation. At a given moment, something comes about that unsettles the control of possibilities and the most general definition of the State. The idea that the State is real oppression has been enormously emphasized but it is, more fundamentally, that which distributes the idea of what is possible and impossible. The event, for its part, will transform what has been declared impossible into a possibility. The possible will be wrested from the impossible. Whence the rallying cry of '68: 'Demand the impossible!' As with all slogans of this type, this was partly excessive and superficial but also extremely profound. 'Demand the impossible' means 'Hold fast to new possibilities, don't force us to return to what has been declared possible or impossible within the established order.' Coming back to your question on political involvement, seizing such possibilities is precisely what it means to be involved in circumstances like these – to accept taking hold of, or, for that matter, being taken hold of, since activity and passivity come to more or less the same thing here. To seize or to be seized by this new possibility, this impossible that is to become real.

– Some say that expecting events alone to yield political truths is a sort of old-fashioned romanticism.

– This view of my philosophy, which tends purely and simply to identify truth and event, is merely a circum-vention. In every situation, there are processes faithful to an event that has previously taken place. It's not a matter, then, of desperately awaiting a miraculous event but, rather, of following through to the very end, to the utmost degree, what you've been able to extract from the previous event and of being as prepared as possible, therefore, to take in subjectively what will inevitably come about. For me, truth is an undertaking; it is a process made possible by the event. The event is only there as a source of possibilities. The possibilities opened up by an event are still present within a situation throughout an entire sequential period. Little by little, they peter out but they are present.

As a result, I still consider myself today as an heir to May '68. May '68 is far behind us, it's forgotten and its traces have almost disappeared. Yet, insofar as I do something, or that I have principles of action, these are in line with what took place then – or more broadly, with what took place in the first half of the 1970s, before the counter-revolution clearly won out.

– If we mustn't wait for the event like an act of grace, how can we prepare for it?

– 'To be prepared for an event' means being subjectively disposed to recognizing new possibilities. Since the event is necessarily unforeseeable given that it doesn't fall under the law of prevailing possibilities, preparing for the event consists in being disposed to welcome it. It's being convinced that the state of things does not set down the most important possibilities, those that open onto the construction of new truths. Being prepared for an event consists in being in a state of mind where one is aware that the order of the world or the prevailing powers don't have absolute control of the possibilities.

How, then, should you prepare yourself? In two ways. First, by remaining faithful to a past event, to the lessons given to the world by that event. This is why the prevailing order fights tooth and nail on this point. It tries to show that past events haven't created any new possibility – hence the discredit cast on all evental episodes. For the last thirty years, one of propaganda's major ploys has consisted in stating that nothing really happened, or, better yet, that what happened, far from creating a new possibility, caused a new horror, a new order or a new regression. The first way to be prepared, then, is to avoid being influenced as far as possible by this kind of propaganda and to seek, instead, what can still sustain a fidelity to past events. It's for this reason that I maintain that political subjects are always between two events. They are never simply confronted with the opposition between the event and the situation but are in a situation upon which events of the recent or distant past still have an impact. The political subject is, then, the interval between the past event and the coming event.

The other way of being prepared, related to the first, is criticism of the established order. Even supposing that the established order is master of the possibilities, it's a matter of showing that these possibilities are, in our view, insufficient. This is a critical task, in a traditional sense, consisting in showing that the system of possibilities offered us is, on a whole series of points, ultimately inhuman. 'Inhuman' in a strict sense: this system does not propose to the social collectivity, to living humanity, possibilities that do justice to that of which it is capable. This criticism will always boil down to showing that the possibilities proposed by the established order do not really mobilize the collectivity's capacities. Of course, this criticism is not an intellectual exercise. It's in practical procedures and in organizations, in the taking-up of positions and in an activism that conserves the memory of things, that fidelity to past events is often found. This criticism tests within society itself the insufficient character of possibilities.

Event and Idea

– What would be, in your view, the new possibilities that could be proposed as preparation for the event?

– Let's start a bit further back. I name 'Idea' that which, regarding a given question, proposes the perspective of a new possibility. The Idea, in politics, is not directly political praxis nor is it a programme; it is not something that is going to be achieved by concrete means. It is rather the possibility in the name of which you act, you transform and you have a programme. It is, then, fairly close to 'principle' – 'act in the name of principles' – but it is more precise. The Idea is really the conviction that a possibility, other than what there is, can come about. The 'event', in the sense we've stated this to involve the creation of a possibility, can very well be said to create an Idea. An Idea is associated with an event because the event is the creation of a possibility and the Idea is the general name of this new possibility. For example, the French Revolution had three major ideas, which are, moreover, often called the 'ideals of the French Republic': namely, liberty, equality and fraternity. The Bolshevik revolution had as Idea communism in power: the proletarian Party-State. From this point of view, the Idea of communism that I talk about today has a different meaning, in terms of which action can be driven by the conviction that another political, collective and social world is possible: a world in no way founded on private property and profit.

– The ideals of the French Revolution are, in sum, very different from the Idea of communism. How are Ideas organized with respect to one another or how do very different events, which are nonetheless all political truths, communicate between themselves?

– Regarding this question, I think in terms of sequences. I think that the Idea forming the vector of insurrections or political innovations changes. During the classical period, which is to say, during the maturation of the French Revolution, the pivotal category is that of liberty. It sets down the norm for equality and property. Liberty, yes, but on condition that it can include the freedom of property or private property. In its turn, property sets down the norm for equality. Equality, yes, but on condition that it does not call into question the rights to private property, which would, in their turn, call into question what is understood by the principles of liberty. A progressive adjustment will, then, give rise to 'formal liberty', which is a juridical framework that is no longer absolute subjection or slavery, in the sense that equality will, from then on, be in keeping with the norm set by this principle of liberty, in the sense that there will no longer be castes or formalized hereditary inequalities – no longer any difference, for example, between nobles and commoners. This adjustment is symbolized by the execution of the king but equally by the fact that property was made sacred. We have here a first configuration.

But there is a second configuration that has not as yet stabilized, in which equality becomes the primordial concept that sets the norm, in its turn, for liberty and property. Equality sets the norm for liberty in the sense that it maintains that liberty must not seriously infringe upon equality. In terms of the norm set by equality, property itself becomes a basis of monstrous injustices, with this leading, as a result, to a priority of collective property over private property.

We are in a political sequence that started, in fact, from the end of the French Revolution, from the compromise between equality, liberty and property, which had no sooner become stable than it was contested. This was the case with the extremists of the French Revolution and with Babeuf and utopian communism. 'Democracy' or 'republic' – even if the two things are not identical – can be said to be the political names adjusted to the first sequence. 'Communism' has to be declared the political name adapted to the second sequence.

Communism

– You are, then, a communist?

– In the sense just mentioned, yes. The communist sequence, in which equality is the key concept that sets the norm for the two others, has a history. My thesis is that we're familiar with two of the stages of this history and that we are in the third. And the problem is, precisely, that we are at the very beginning of the third and don't, therefore, know very much about it yet! The communist Idea in its modern form – for it is already present with Plato – emerged in the nineteenth century. It signified a historical outcome of class struggle in terms of the disappearance of private property. This is the chief idea of communism for Marx's *Manifesto*: the abolition of private property, which amounts to the triumph of equality over the historical connection between property and liberty. The French Revolution, for its part, said 'yes' to liberty but on condition that equality be subordinated to the liberty of property.

The Marxist thematic makes communism, then, an ideology of equality – with class struggle being that which the real consists of – that comes into play around the question of the property of the means of production. With regard to the first stage of communism set down by Marx, communism is a historical category. Marx subordinated politics to history, communism being the Idea that was going to be accomplished, historically, when class struggle came to an end. He was profoundly convinced that the class struggle between the bourgeoisie and the proletariat would be the last such struggle, after those between patricians and plebeians and between nobles and bourgeois. 'Communism' became for him the result of that ultimate historical confrontation. It was in no way the ideal programme, replete with details and all, of a society freed from all past obstructions. That, for him, was 'utopian communism'.

In fact, rather than an opposition of scientific communism and utopian communism, Marx contra Fourier, we have historical communism contra communism as a pure ideal. Marx's big idea was that communism would come about in a relatively short period, when the proletariat was sufficiently organized to smash the machine of the bourgeois State. A vast movement was going to carry it. It is very interesting to note that Marx defines the communist party as a simple party of the workers' movement in general. He wasn't thinking of a separate organization. The workers' movement had within it people who had communist ideas, those who knew where the movement was headed as a whole. From this point of view, the test of Paris Commune was to be crucial. It was to show that this vision in terms of insurrectional movements runs up against resistances that Marx had neither thematized nor envisaged: capitalism's defensive sturdiness was, indeed, decidedly more forceful than foreseen, and imperialism was to develop totally new means of corrupting the working class.

We enter progressively, then, into the second stage, which is completely centred on the question of

organization. 'Communism' is no longer the name of
the general Idea of emancipation but the goal of particular organizations responsible for ensuring that the
popular insurrection really and truly triumphs. Everything becomes subordinated to the efficiency of these
organizations. They are still named communist because
they fit within the schema we've described – the primacy
of equality over liberty and property – but they are,
above all, instrumental. The idea of Lenin was to dispel
forever the spectre of the failure of the Paris Commune.
Never again a seizure of power paid ultimately by the
complete triumph of the adversaries, the annihilation
of our forces and the massacre of twenty thousand
workers in our streets! We have to win. The fundamental category of the second stage is 'victory' and this is
what was to fill millions of people with enthusiasm: the
victory of the October Revolution. For the seizure of
power was to take place. Interestingly, 'communism' is
expressed from then on largely in the form of adjectives,
as with 'communist parties', 'socialist States' and 'communist militants'.

The organization found itself, as a result, fetishized,
being attributed a transcendence as the absolute instru-
ment of victory, with which it had become one. Think
back to a declaration of the period like 'The Party is
always right.' The Party was historical reason. For
Marx, historical reason was considerably broader, being
the historical movement that bore communism, whereas
that which was to bear communism henceforth was the
communist organization. There is, then, an extremely
violent fetishization and statization of the Idea that was
to dominate the communist undertaking of the twentieth century. This was to consist in taking power and it
would be identified with forms of power.

– Isn't it here that the fundamental difference between
Stalin and Mao becomes apparent?

– Stalin is the proper name of the absolutely statized form of the communist Idea, the name of the great socialist dictatorship. During the twentieth century, there were great socialist dictatorships that claimed to be representative of communism in a form that was wholly that of absolute State sovereignty. This State was itself directly the product of the party. One had, therefore, the 'Party-State' as communism's centre of gravity, represented by a proper name.

How could one justify the communist idea being represented by a Party-State that is never anything other than a particular construction and without the historical legitimacy that Marx saw in the communist Idea? It was necessary to maintain that this Party-State was the representative of the general movement, and hence of the proletariat, and to put in place an extraordinarily metaphysical doctrine of representation: the Party-State represents the proletariat. This was not at all the idea of Marx, for whom the communists were only a section of the general workers' movement. In these great dictatorships the relation was inversed: there is only the Party-State and whosoever is outside this is outside the representation of the general movement. Finally, the Party-State itself needs to be represented, for its key is representation. The proper name, Stalin, represents, then, the Party-State, since it is necessary to arrive at the supreme, absolute One – to arrive, as in monarchies, at the One of a body. Stalin is the name of this process.

Mao is something completely different. To identify him with Stalin is a serious error. Mao perfectly understood that the Party-State was inappropriate because it had shown itself powerless to organize true equality. It had been victorious, but it had become, in its victory, the main obstacle to moving further ahead. By declaring 'Without the communist movement, there is no communism', Mao returned in a certain sense to Marx's conception. Communism can only be a movement, it cannot be a State. In reality, 'communist State' is an oxymoron, an absurdity. Mao therefore put things together as best he could and tried to relaunch a movement. But against what? Against the State, and thus against the Communist Party itself. That's what the Cultural Revolution was: the working and student masses flung against the State, which, by bringing about an inextricable situation of anarchy and destruction, along with the emergence of innumerable factions, ultimately led to the intervention of the army. Mao lashed out at the very essence of that of which he was the product: the idea that the representation of the movement is assured by the Party-State. Yet, if, without any other idea than that, one relaunches the movement against the latter, what one creates is extraordinary anarchy! Mao was at least conscious that the communist question could no longer be that of State representation of the movement.

The Cultural Revolution and its failure close the second stage. It is established that not only did the Party-State lead, under Stalin, to terror as the sole means of governing, but also that there is no way of rectifying the situation by simply appealing to spontaneous movements of the masses. Even if the signifier Mao floated above all that as the signifier confounding the Party and the movement, what it brought about was nevertheless total confusion. It's an extraordinary episode – everyone could claim to represent Mao and brandish red flag against red flag – but it thoroughly closes the period: one has to go beyond representation by the Party-State.

– Nothing is more terrible than the figure of Mao in the collective imaginary today. He would seem to be one of the great criminals of history.

– Twentieth-century revolutionary politics never claimed to be democratic and respect freedoms, etcetera. That was not their norm. They undertook, for the first time in history, to subordinate the terms of liberty and property, and their internal connection, to an egalitarian norm borne by popular forces. They explicitly presented themselves as dictatorships, as with 'the dictatorship of the proletariat'. They designated violence as one of the means of their action, one of the conditions of their victory. This modality has its own coherence, founded on the necessity – which is also that on which it wagers – of creating a new world. The perspective is that of bringing into being, by all possible means, a new world. It is absurd to compare this, from the standpoint of general norms of action, with the parliamentary regime of a minor and peaceful power like France today. The revolution, stated Mao, is not a gala dinner.

At the same time, we have countless texts by Mao in which he recalls that it is necessary to economize human forces – contrary to Stalin. There are lots of accounts that attest to the way in which he conducted himself with ordinary soldiers, especially during the Long March. He imposed, for example, the obligation of giving speeches and organizing ceremonies in honour of anyone who had fallen, even if they were a cook or a simple soldier. Mao, who never ceased making war, thought of the revolution in terms of war but he also insisted on everyone being respected for who they are. He was extremely attentive to what he called 'the resolution of contradictions among the people': for example, how to relate to people, the relations between people, the form of meetings, and popular power.

To consider Mao a 'terrible' figure is a particularly bad choice of adjective given his appreciation of popular forms of conviviality, his penchant for humour. This figure is not Stalin. Mao was an approachable person, always smiling. He was even made fun of for his taste for jokes. The image of Mao fabricated today is completely in keeping with counter-revolutionary procedures. It resembles more and more the way Robespierre was hauled over the coals as morbid, withdrawn, and cold as ice. There is, in truth, a whole book to write on the way revolutionaries are portrayed in counter-revolutionary literature: Robespierre, Stalin, Mao and Lenin himself are all put through the mill. The same thing has even been tried with Marx, who was hardly, after all, a certified blood drinker. There are books that denounce him for having slept with his maid! In sum, the counter-revolutionary propaganda is doing its job. And it is crucial, for it, to definitively discredit revolutionary episodes and the proper names associated with them. Yet, even someone as moderate and as 'republican' as Clémenceau, who was someone who violently smashed workers' strikes, ended up saying that the Revolution was for him a single block, such that one couldn't state, without ultimately giving reason to the established counter-revolutionaries, that Danton was Good and Robespierre Evil. The communist experience is also a single block. This doesn't mean that everything about it was good, but simply that it is necessary to come to terms with this period. If you don't come to terms with it you ratify the adversary's propaganda.

– Let's come to terms, then, with the epoch, with the past. For all that, though, what future is there for communism?

– We are faced with an alternative: either the category of communism has to be abandoned or we enter a third stage. This is a clear choice, which presupposes revising and re-elaborating the category of communism and the relations between this category and political processes. It's a crucial choice. For my part, I choose the second option, that of a third stage of communism. I don't see how it is possible to say that the communist Idea has to be abandoned without finding oneself fully within the consensus. This consensus has a name: 'democracy'. One can try to go with this and oppose a 'true'

democracy to a 'false' democracy but I think that this
is a weak position. It's necessary to restate that we are
still in the sequence opened up by the French Revolution
and that there have been two stages of the communist
Idea, that of the nineteenth century exemplified by Marx
and that of the communist parties. We can undertake
an evaluation of these two stages. It's not up to our
enemies to do this but up to us. Yet we know that we
have to go further than this. It is, in any case, more
efficient and far more promising, if one wants to prepare
for the political events that will not fail to occur, to
remain faithful to the word 'communism'. Certain
words have, in fact, been corrupted by being incorporated within consensus, with the only possible rival to
the word communism being, for that matter, 'democracy'. Democracy? One day, no doubt, this word will
be salvaged. But it will be salvaged by going from communism to democracy and not vice versa.

Coming back to the concrete situation: Sarkozy, Israel, Europe

– You denounce Sarkozy's 'barbarism'. There wouldn't,
then, be a Maoist barbarism strictly speaking but there
would be a Sarkozian one. Such a proposition, if it is
indeed yours, will not fail to shock a lot of people.

– With Sarkozy, it's something else all the same, and the
criteria that have to be applied to him are, first of all,
those he himself purports to privilege. We are, here,
dealing with consensus, the consensus around capitalism and parliamentary democracy. This is a society that
alleges to be essentially pacific and ethical, the only possible model of justice and public morality. Now, I maintain that Sarkozy is in no way the model of his own
norms. If he made himself out to be a great revolutionary purporting to change the world by overturning the

old feudal classes and creating a socialist economy, I wouldn't apply the same criteria to him.

There is no ethics in general, as I've argued in a book precisely entitled *Ethics*.[5] There isn't any overarching, divine ethics that would be the equivalent to the ten commandments of a God. There are ethics of particular processes. There are situations and there are truths. The norms and principles in the name of which one intervenes are internal to these situations. To compare Sarkozy and Mao as if there were, between them, a common, universal, ethical space that doesn't have to take account of situations, is preposterous; it's really like comparing chalk and cheese. I refuse to do it.

I take Sarkozy at face value, as a president elected in a parliamentary regime. I ask myself: 'what's he got in store for us?' 'What does he want from me?' If Mao summoned me to become a soldier of the revolution, I would think about it. But a summons from Sarkozy is something I don't want any part of. And there is, undoubtedly, a Sarkozian barbarism. It doesn't consist for the moment in having people shot. But it, nevertheless, treats many people very badly and promotes insupportable forms of contempt. I know, from my own real experience, how youths are treated today. I know how workers of African origin are treated. I know this little spoken-of, half-said and badly said reality very well. I also know how Sarkozy speaks of intellectuals, knowledge and the arts, as well as of the mad, delinquents and 'perverts'. All of which, in the world as it is, is barbarian: there's no other word for it.

– At a conference in Buenos Aires, you declared yourself for a fusion between France and Germany. Are you

---

[5] *Ethics. An Essay on the Understanding of Evil*, trans. Peter Hallward, London and New York, Verso, 2001. Originally published as: *L'éthique*, Paris, Hatier, 1993.

inventing a new genre of political philosophy, that of political-fiction?

– This is my counterproposal – of a – State, to the present European construction. The latter is bogged down because of the attempt to create a whole out of bits and pieces whose sole principle of unity will, in reality, be the laws of contemporary capitalism. Brussels is an executive power of this capitalism's requirements. The political counterbalance is insufficient. Considering the history of Europe, I do not see any other counterbalance than attempting to create a European power comparable to the superpowers that are emerging, such as China, the new Russia that will end up hauling itself out of its present stagnation, or Brazil. Europe will remain totally powerless as long as it is merely a conglomeration of middling powers, whose only common interest is the development of globalized capitalism. A political invention is called for!

For historical, philosophical and spiritual reasons, the most realistic but also the most interesting possibility is to create a single State zone formed of France and Germany. Contrasting the two has always been crucial in Europe. German progressives have always looked towards France, while the French interested in profound aesthetic or philosophical insight have always looked towards Germany. The fusion, or the creation, in other words, of a single zone of power, would, then, be fully productive. The world order would be changed by it. France + Germany would make up a great power.

I recognize it's a provocative idea. Preposterous, some would say. But this idea has a long history, including in bourgeois politics. De Gaulle, not giving a damn about the rest of Europe, considered Adenauer to be his partner. It was somewhat the same between Mitterrand and Kohl. Even Sarkozy and Angela Merkel have tried to set the tone for how to deal with the crisis. There

was also the common refusal by Chirac and Schroeder
to become involved in Iraq. This sketches the history of
a privileged partnership.

That's why the idea of putting an end, at the same
time and with a single stroke, to France and Germany
is, after all, a rather interesting one. These two countries
are at the end of their tether. France was a great imperial
power that is now minor, while Germany is a country
that has never known what it was, and which has
sought, in what are ultimately terrifying ventures,
to find its identity. Germany could, then, be freed
from this question of identity at the same time as France
would rid itself of an arrogance that is no longer appropriate. This Germano-France or this Franco-Germany
would be the emergence of an absolutely new figure in
the world.

– A polemic raised by a number of personalities in
journalism and academia raged full-bore following the
publication of your text, 'Uses of the Word "Jew"'.[6] If
one is to believe them, you are then, Alain Badiou,
'anti-Semitic'.

– This book was a collection of texts that I'd written
over twenty years. It wasn't at all a new stance. My aim
wasn't so much to talk about the Israeli–Palestinian
conflict as to examine the ideological role assigned to
this issue and, above all, to the Holocaust – or the Shoah
– in the ideological debate taking place within France.
It was a matter of examining a point of view that
amounts, first, to reducing politics to morality, and,

---

[6] 'Uses of the Word "Jew"', in Alain Badiou, *Polemics*, trans. Steven
Corcoran, New York, Verso, 2006. Originally published in Alain
Badiou and Cécile Winter, *Circonstances*, 3, Paris, Lignes, Léo
Scheer, 2005.

second, to a total re-westernization of politics, with it having the added bonus of restoring the legitimacy of a certain dependence vis-à-vis the United States. All of which converged towards the denunciation of what we can observe: the total instrumentalization of the word 'Jew'. Many Jews accept this instrumentalization. They are wrong to do so. It is not good for them or anyone else.

I wanted, then, to raise the question of 'Why has this name brought back, especially among French intellectuals and, singularly, those coming from extreme Left, and even Maoist, perspectives, that which was believed to be the enemy of any emancipatory politics: namely, the question of identity?'[7] That's the problem: the return of the question of identity in the field of politics believed to be emancipatory ones. Now, an emancipatory politics tries to go beyond questions of identity. While reactionary, and particularly fascist, politics are always ferociously identitarian, it seemed, all the same, clear to me that emancipatory politics were universalist!

The return to identitarianism on the part of people coming from the camp of the revolution was guided by the word 'Jew', which produced, after all, the Islamophobia whose catastrophic consequences we are seeing today. Here, then, is one negative consequence of this defence of identity. I have seen develop, even among close friends, a theme of the 'war of civilizations' that is not only reactive but grotesque. Certain well-known thinkers, much in the media, have brandished a conception of Jewish or French identity against an Arab identity. As though this is the main debate today! When politics strays into identities, it is lost. It sets the ground for nothing other than wars, civil wars and horrors.

[7] Ibid.

I've always considered that the word 'Jew' was, among identities, that most related to universalism. I have always seen it like that, along with my Jewish friends. One only has to think of all the Jews who have participated in revolutionary movements. Fully accepting themselves as Jews, they considered 'Jew' to be one of the names by which national or communitarian identities were shifted by being projected towards universalism. I was, therefore, stupefied by the abrupt inversion of the word 'Jew' in the opposite direction, towards identity and the apologia of an identitarian State, the so-called 'Jewish State'. Pétain, in the case of France, was to manufacture, through collaboration and total oppression, the phantom of a 'French State'. No State with such an adjective at its sides is acceptable today.

– Isn't the return of this question of Jewish identity a simple effect of the Israeli–Palestinian problem?

– My point of view is that the Israeli–Palestinian question should not be posed in terms of neo-colonialism. My point of view, which concurs with that of most of my Israeli friends, is that neither the thesis which is manifestly that of the Israeli government ('the less we hear speak of the Palestinians, the better it is'), nor even the thesis, consensual on the Left, of two States, outlines a future for anyone at all. The latter thesis is, moreover – as is patently evident to everyone – less and less viable. The pacific and universalist schema is that of a binational State in which Jews and Arabs would co-exist. They already, moreover, largely live together. One has to stop telling us fibs: they aren't separated by terrifying identities that would necessitate a wall for them to be able to live in peace. They are a lot closer to one another than are, in Switzerland, the Protestants of the Vaud canton and the Catholics in the remotest parts of Valais. And Switzerland is one of the oldest States in Europe. . . .

In reality, I'm a moderate on the question. Of course, the Jews are in Palestine and are going to stay there. There's no need to brandish against them an Islamic ideology, as does a good part of Hamas, which has set about making the situation even worse. I'm for the creation of a space common to the two peoples; I'm for the formula of an invented State. I've always thought that had there been a great Israeli politician, an authentic visionary, he would have invited Arafat into his government. What we saw in South Africa was, moreover, a bit like this.

I must admit it is extraordinarily unpleasant that a clique, whose centre of gravity is, unfortunately, the review *Les Temps Modernes*, decided to launch a campaign against me claiming I was anti-Semitic. Nonetheless, I can clearly see the reason for this despicable attack, since an 'anti-Semite' for them isn't, as one might have expected, someone who is against Jews but someone who doesn't use the word 'Jew' in exactly the same way they do. The clique in question has no other goal than becoming the owners of the word. For them, 'Jew' can only be an identity, an identity that has the right to absolute respect because of the Shoah and which must be recognized as being at the basis of the State of Israel, with this leading, as a result, to unconditional support for that State. Whosoever doesn't partake of this configuration is an anti-Semite. I wanted to break this taboo by noting, firstly, that the historical relation between the word 'Jew' and universalism, including in its revolutionary form, is crucial, and, secondly, that the key to the extermination of European Jews doesn't lie in Jewish identity but in the use of the word 'Jew' within a criminal politics that sprung up and was implemented in Europe under the conditions of modern capitalism: namely, Nazism. It's this politics that was, for its part, ferociously identitarian! I took the risk of stepping forward under fire from those who had called me an anti-Semite. But I gave as good as I got. To be called a

Maoist is a matter of indifference to me. That comes from people who don't know what the word means. But to be called an anti-Semite, that's something I will not tolerate.

– This question of Jewish identity, brings us, perhaps, to the religious question. Some give this question a primordial importance in the political analysis of our time. It's true that it's particularly Islam which is targeted. I'm reminded of a remark by Lenin on art, according to which, in periods of political inactivity, art is at best a mixture of mysticism and pornography. Can one generalize? Does our age waver between mysticism and pornography?

– My position on religions is not at all the one that is dominant today, according to which the religious question has become very important again, with our having gone back to a great epoch of religious conflicts, of a war of civilizations. For my part, I am a strict Nietzschean on this question. I really think that God is dead. If he is dead, he's dead. You have to take it seriously. The 'return of religion' masks, then, something else, I'm absolutely convinced of this. Religion is, in fact, the mask of political decomposition. Which isn't to say that its living. Every mask, in a sense, is a death mask.

Under the usurped name of religion, and under the disguise of a dead god, what exists is tradition. The Islamists do not propose a new vision of God. They speak about women's clothing, dietary habits and traditional law, opposing all that to Coca-Cola, short skirts and so on. Where is religion in all this? There is only tradition, such as this is maintained in rural regions, country towns, and a fringe of the uprooted and impoverished populations; a tradition that is systematized by small groups of hyper-reactionary intellectuals, be they

American neo-conservatives or Islamic fundamentalists, who are, moreover, at the fundament of nothing. Facing this hardline tradition that is itself decadent, what exactly do we find braced under the no less usurped names of 'freedom' and 'democracy'? Well, nothing less, if you so please, than pornography. Ultimately, what one claims to be a war between religions is a fairly pathetic combat between tradition and pornography.

I think that the alleged confrontation between the West and Islam, the West and terrorist barbarism – alleged in a sense, but all too real in another – is, in fact, internal to the whole of human existence today. It's the confrontation between tradition and merchandise. This doesn't prevent interferences between the two: one knows that some of those who instrumentalize tradition are very well set up in the world of merchandise. Let's not try to make us believe that the traffickers of Saudi Arabia are mystics and models of piety. They are people doing business, like everyone else, and who instrumentalize tradition in order to reinforce their position in their business deals. God, in all that, is totally cadaveric. He's more dead than dead!

Those who continue to cling to the question of religions are clinging on to something of an altogether phantasmatic nature. The situation is far more serious than that. If it were only a combat between secularism and religion! People are acting as though we found ourselves in the 1890s and the world was embroiled in a violent quarrel between free-thinkers and priests. The obsolete character of this vision is absolutely frightening. There are people who consider the historical combat of our time to consist in determining whether women should or should not cover their hair with scarves, just as there are populations who enthusiastically vote against the construction of minarets in European cities! To borrow an expression from the past, it's enough to make you roll on the floor and kick your legs in consternation![8] All these questions of customs or anti-customs are completely coded by things that have nothing to do with any Idea whatsoever. Some say to me 'Think of the republican pact! In collective co-existence it's necessary to show one's face, and so on.' What a joke! I'm tempted to reply to them that I, personally, don't have any desire to show my face to all the jerks that govern us. At least the English reject the burka for police-related reasons that are, ultimately, more honest; the rationale being that it can serve as a disguise for people with bombs! But to make it a question of civilization, the burning issue of today, is simply ridiculous. When one thinks of the situation in Palestine, the preparations for war against Iran, the occupation of Afghanistan, the millions of unemployed generated by the financial crisis, the destuction of the public services the villainous laws in France against family reunification for foreign workers, the rise throughout Europe of Austrian small-town racism and chauvinism, and when one sees Islamophobes bewailing the death of our 'civilization', one says to oneself that the world seriously needs a massive dose of communism.

– I understand better, as a result, your taking a stance against the ban on the so-called Islamic headscarf even though you lay claim to the non-religious tradition of materialism.

---

[8] 'The expression from the past' that Badiou borrows here is, in fact, an expression gleaned from a text by the French poet Isidore Ducasse, who published under the pseudonym of Comte de Lautréamont. In a passage of his *Poésies 1* (1870), Lautréamont recalls the extreme consternation he felt as a child on reading Jacques-Henri Bernardin de Saint-Pierre's novel, *Paul et Virginie*. So bleak did the young Lautréamont find this book, so contrary to all his hopes for happiness, that 'it made him gnash his teeth and roll on the floor, kicking all the while his wooden horse' in irritation. Rather than include the literal translation of this expression in the text, we have opted for a more general formulation. [Translator's note]

– I am, indeed, absolutely opposed to this kind of decision which is of the order of a derisory manipulation of
public opinion. One singles out an imaginary enemy,
whereas, insofar as there is, today, an enemy, this consists of those who have real powers, those wielding
capitalist power. There is no other. I am against any
endeavour that would have us believe that the enemy
are the religious or scarves on women's hair or con-
cealed faces. These are absolutely patent operations of
diversion and alienation. They divert us from confront-
ing the real enemy. Given the opposition of tradition
and merchandise, to pretend that the enemy is tradition
consists simply in rallying oneself behind merchandise.
We are all very aware that libertinage and tradition are
structurally in conflict, but this doesn't furnish any way
of forging any form of politics dealing with human
emancipation. There is, then, today an overt, and weari-
some, way of amusing the crowd with inexistent problems. We are in a crisis of politics, a crisis of the Idea
in the sense I've defined above. We are already powerless enough as it is, alas, in the face of real enemies
without us falling for imaginary ones.

– Are there other cases of smoke and mirrors for our
time?

– Between us, I think much the same of environmental-
ism. It's a very powerful ideology. I intend to write
on this issue one day, just as a way of getting into hot
water again! The idea of everyone uniting to save the
planet is, after all, rather crude. It's to advocate exactly
the same position as the nationalism of the early
twentieth century. In this case, too, it was: 'All United!'
'All united, beyond our class differences, against the
Huns!' It was a very convenient way to avoid recognizing that the main adversary was an internal one.
The analogy is striking: 'Yes, of course, there are
enormous disparities, poor countries and rich ones,

bourgeois and workers . . . But all united in the face of
global warming!' Brecht would have written a play in
which the chorus of people would bleat 'Let us save the
planet! Let us save the planet!', while the swindlers got
ever richer.

– But couldn't the dangers heralded by global warming
lead humanity to exercise greater control of itself or,
even, to a radical transformation?

– Let's first note, as regards the possibility of global
warming, that no proof has been established. Environ-
mentalist propaganda compresses predictions of development that bear on half a century and makes out as
though there will be a catastrophe within a year. If sea
levels rise as a result of global warming, this is not going
to happen from one day to the next. There will be a
constant and continual effort to counter this effect in
order to adapt to the changes. We can, doubtlessly,
expect populations to be displaced. This has happened
many times before and humanity has endured things
infinitely more serious and radical than those which are
being forecast now. It underwent an ice age and managed
to survive with the means at its disposal – which were
not at all those we have today.
    I think that, with environmentalism, we're dealing
with a millenarianism. I'm not seeking to deny global
warming (not being a climate expert), nor the necessity
of becoming more disciplined in our practices. I'm
against transforming these phenomena into ideology.
Ideology assumes here a familiar form, that of millenarianism or the belief in a final great catastrophe. A large
number of the films produced in Hollywood are about
nothing else. This ideology generates a state of mind
that is both terrified and powerless. Now, nothing is
more favourable to those in power than the mixture of
terror and powerlessness. It's the best possible state for
populations from the point of view of the powers we

are subjected to today, which, under their democratic rags, are extraordinarily violent and tyrannical. These visions of final catastrophe tend to mobilize everyone to conserve the planet just as it is, with its temperature, its pleasant 'environment' for the petit-bourgeoisie of rich countries, and its predators of globalized capitalism. But the truth, concerning what interests me about the 'planet', is that hundreds of millions of people are on the brink of starvation, that savage and absurd wars are being conducted all over the world, that a total stupefaction of populations is spreading under the reign of merchandise, and that all of this will inevitably lead one day to totally cataclysmic crises and wars. We have to destroy capital's domination, extricate ourselves from its 'democratic' propaganda, and concentrate our, already extremely limited, forces on this point, rather than making deals with green banks on account of the climate.

That said, in today's situation, characterized by both a radical weakness of emancipatory politics and the obscure combat between tradition and merchandise, everything could well deteriorate. There is not an operative rationality capable of controlling the trends that might be provoked by a catastrophe, the displacement of populations or a national affair that goes wrong. The situation in the Middle East alone is capable of sparking off a nuclear war. This shows the extreme weakness, today, of what I call the Idea. Without the Idea, the only thing left is an animalized humanity. Capitalism is the animalization of the human beast, who no longer lives except in terms of its interests and what it deems to be its due. This animalization is extremely dangerous because it is devoid of values and laws. If humanity does not work towards its own unfurling, its own invention, it has, effectively, no other option than to work towards its destruction. That which is not under the reign of the Idea is under the reign of death. It is not an anodyne matter for the human species to be animal. Humanity is the species that has need of the Idea in order to dwell reasonably in its own world.

Perspectives

– Finally, what is to be done? Is, for example, a certain relationship to civil disobedience or to breaking the law acceptable today?

– It seems to me that an answer to this question consists of three levels and not one alone. First, I think that strictly ideological questions have a great importance. We are coming out of a particular sequence of the history of revolutions and States. There is always in a case like this a type of new beginning or necessary step backwards that causes fundamental debates to resurge. We have to ask ourselves a very simple question: is there really, strategically, a vision or possibility of organizing the human collectivity that is radically different from that which exists today? This problem must absolutely be tackled head-on and for itself. If any serious uncertainty lingers on this subject, the only possible outcome is an inevitable return to the existing order. In my terms, this is what I call the question of communism – but other names are possible. It's a question, in any case, of whether or not an authentic global alternative exists as regards the destiny of human history.

We need to recall that for Marx, and in this particular case also Rosa Luxembourg, the alternative was socialism or barbarism. The question raised was also that of the effective time span of human civilization. This question has to be readdressed, which implies considerable effort. It would be wrong to believe that this kind of work is exclusively the reserve of intellectuals since the conviction that something else exists has to become a popular conviction at some stage or another. It cannot remain a strictly intellectual construction.

When ideas take hold of the masses, Mao used to say, they become like a spiritual atomic bomb.

The question of spiritual atom bombs poses itself today more than ever. The least one can say is that, for the instant, our spiritual nuclear power is very limited. And so, that's the situation for the first level, which is the level of public debate and the capacity to maintain a point of view head-on.

Let's turn to the second level. This is that of collective experimentation, with this political experimentation being at an inevitably local scale today because we have neither the slightest idea nor the slightest concept of what might be a general movement. In the previous period, the global movement was designated by a precise term, that of 'revolution', 'proletarian' or 'socialist'. We no longer have any equivalent concept. We don't know today what a revolution or the figure of the State corresponding to this could be. All we can undertake are local experimentations during the time it takes to progressively find more general categories. This experimentation must be guided by ideological norms. The two points are, then, absolutely linked. It's a question of whether what one does in a particular situation goes in the direction of equality, elaborating a vision that is opposed to the absolute domination of private property and of the political and social organization that depends on this. It is possible to try out, in very specific situations, points that serve to verify communist principles. Some of these are more advanced than others today. Thus, the work on the fate reserved to foreign workers has given rise to fully arrayed experimentations. However, on other issues such as public health or internationalism, things are much less clear.

As for the third level, this relates, given the first two points – a retransformed ideological conviction and significant local experimentations – to where we're at vis-à-vis the question of organization. The monumental and, in its own way, terrorizing, figure of the party – in

the sense that it dominated the revolution during the
twentieth century – is manifestly no longer capable of
seducing, mobilizing or organizing people. Yet, the
question of organization remains central.

– What is to be done, then?

– Let me resume by way of a synthesis. An ideological
effort to reconstitute the living Idea of a general alternative to the existing order, situated experimentations
that are confrontational – and can include practices
of disobedience and infringement – and finally, a pro-
longed meditation, equally involving experimentation,
on the question of organization. This, then, would be
my 'What is to be done?'

2

Love

Love versus politics

– Turning now to love, we might start off from Hannah Arendt's declaration in *The Human Condition* that, because 'of its inherent worldlessness, love can only become false and perverted when it is used for political purposes such as the change or salvation of the world.'[1] This allows us at the same time to make a transition. Is there anything you'd like to say about this quotation? What do you understand by 'amorous condition'?

– Love is essentially when there are two, rather than one, who experientially experiment with the world. Love is in no way formed, then, through a reduction of two to one. This is the romantic, fusional conception of lovers' merging in a supreme, ecstatic unity whose only truth is death, as illustrated by Tristan and Isolde. I think, on the contrary, that love splits each individual's narcissistic unity in such a way that it opens up an

[1] Arendt, Hannah, *The Human Condition*, Chicago and London, University of Chicago Press, /1958/ 1998, p. 52.

experience of the world that is taken on as the experience of the two. I've named love the 'scene of the Two'.
Whereas politics takes difference as its material and
attempts to construct a minimal operative unity within
this element, love, on the contrary, shatters the primary
units and establishes the reign of the Two over the
experience of the world.

It's for this reason I state that love begins where politics ends, which seems to me to validate what Hannah
Arendt says. I'm very wary of the category of love being
used in any way in the field of the collectivity. This is
what religion does. Moreover, religion uses love in order
to polarize this field and rearrange it in terms of the love
of transcendence. When all is said and done, it's the love
we have for God, or God for us, that is the key to everything, with love thereby being instrumentalized in the
service of transcendence. It is striking, moreover, that
love as much as terror, or a mixture of the two, can be
instrumentalized in the service of transcendence. From
this point of view, the great dictatorships are isomorphic
with the great religions. The relationship to the 'little
father of the people' consisted of an extraordinary love,
on the one hand, and of absolute terror on the other.
Both were real and in no way made up. The overwhelm-
ing majority of Soviet citizens really felt an immense love
for Stalin. When he died, there was a collective mourn-
ing of gigantic proportions. It is also true that there was
an absolute reign of fear. Such an indiscernibility of love
and terror is an intrinsic part of religion's authority,
though it is also, unfortunately, something that wreaks
havoc at times in people's private lives.

– You go so far as to state that politics begins where
love ends.

– When I said that love begins where politics ends, it
was on the basis of what is, in fact, a fairly formal,
almost algebraic analysis. Ultimately, the position of
that which is united, or which is one, is always a result

in politics. Politics starts from the infinite multiplicity; more precisely, it starts from the fact that the infinite multiplicity that popular affirmation presents is essentially different from the type of infinity represented by power and the State. The starting event of all politics is this type of double infinity – the infinity of popular presentation and the infinity of state representation, to take up here the categories of *Being and Event*. In the end, it's always a question of the way in which popular infinity must be able to curb, norm, and tendentially weaken or dissolve despotic state power. That which at first takes the form of separation and multiplicities, communication difficulties and internal divisions, leads bit by bit – sequence after sequence – to the construction of forms of unity.

The other way I also put this is that it's not the problem of difference that is constitutive. Difference is what there is. People, as well as nations, are necessarily different. The problem is to know how to produce sameness. This is a very important point. We've come out of a period of the cult of difference that was, ultimately, fairly negative. A truly great politics aims, rather, at producing a unity with a differentiated material. This was, after all, the supreme goal of internationalism: there are cultures, civilizations, and nations, but ultimately you have to set yourself up at the point where all that doesn't prevent you from acting together politically. Politics goes, then, from diversity to the same, whereas love consists, on the contrary, in constructing a difference that is accepted as a unique path. Politics goes from difference to the same, love introduces difference into the same.

The event-encounter and constructing the scene of the Two

– If one tries to set out the way your general theory of the subject and truth connects with this condition that is love, it's clear that love begins with an event, that of the encounter. Does this mean that there is love only when it's love at first sight?

– Love at first sight is a way of poeticizing the encounter, a way of describing it in a somewhat emphatic and, it must be said, retroactive style – as with evocations of its bedazzling character, for instance. In some cases, this can be true. You're somewhere, you see a woman arrive, and all of a sudden something absolutely oscillates in your representation of the world. This is not entirely an invention. What's constant, in any case – love at first sight or not – is an element of contingency. This element of the encounter, this ineluctable element, is the beginning of everything. It is almost nothing, just as is, basically, every event. An event is, in general, almost nothing: it appears at the same time as it disappears; it's not immediately evident that it has any future at all, and it can't at first be deciphered as regards its consequences.

Love is a good example: I'm introduced to a co-worker from the office or someone else. What we're dealing with is almost minimal. Sometimes it happens that you feel right away that it's important. On other occasions, you feel nothing at all like this at the time. There are loads of variations in this domain. What interests me here is the contingency. It's striking to see that this pure contingency of the amorous origin, in its contradiction with the logic of arranged marriage as a symbol of that which is precisely not contingent, was represented very early on, especially in the theatre. The simple fact of 'boy meeting girl', through an exchange of glances in the street or at church, is pitted by the theatre against the social machinery that, for its part, has foreseen the solid forging of ones within a well-constructed two. This contradiction between an absolutely contingent origin and an absolutely prepared one is an inexhaustible theme for the theatre. For my part,

I often give love as an example of an event. On the face of things, an amorous encounter is nothing at all. Nietzsche wasn't completely wrong to say that important events are ushered in 'on doves' feet'. It's almost nothing and yet it can be the start of a fabulous story.

– You insist, however, on the procedure that follows, the amorous 'labour' as you put it, all while refusing a transcendental vision of this procedure and maintaining that it's not a question of illusion but of a productive reality.

– Obviously, if love was merely a sort of mechanical consequence of the contingency – this almost non-existent something – at the start, then it would be impossible to grasp its true nature. We wouldn't understand that it involves a succession of choices and deliberations, dramas and expectations, of trying things out and rectifying what happens. But everyone knows that there comes a moment when the encounter is sealed by the declaration: 'I love you.' Once the encounter is determined in the declaration, whatever form this may take, the amorous experience in the strict sense begins: that of a world 'existed' by two. There'll be question of moving into an apartment, with space itself having to become a space for two. Time too, for its part, is to be a time for two: when are we going to see each other . . . and when not? Are we going on holidays together? Little by little, a series of elements of everyday life are taken up, captured, by this salience of being-two. All these elements have to be included within the scene of the Two. This is not something that comes about naturally. They have to be made to enter into this scene, with your being brought up against points that can be crucial: having a child or not, for example. All these things make up the content of the amorous procedure. This is what the reality of love is. If you reduce it to a psychological state, you're not going to understand much. Of course, there is the psychological state of one and the other partner. Yet, ultimately, what all that comes down to is a shared experience that can't be reduced to either the psychology or the individual narcissism of the members of the couple. As is well known, narcissism, or inevitable egoism, is usually much more of a hindrance than a help when it comes to the unfolding of the amorous figure. Love is not a negotiation between two egoisms, it's not a contract. There is, in this case, no instance of arbitration. We are dealing with an immanence but the immanence of a construction – that of the scene of the Two itself.

This is why love is creative. It constructs a singular experience of difference. This is a unique, radical, intense and vital experience, to the point that the difficulties it encounters, the threats of its interruption, are dramatic. I never fail to recall that love is a bloody procedure that can generate acts of violence and murder. It's comparable, from this point of view, to politics. In love, it's a matter of only two and not millions, but there is nevertheless a great number of crises, a great number of losses, and a considerable amount of suffering. Love is a creative undertaking and nothing that is creative is easy. Yet in love (as in politics), there are extraordinary moments of enthusiasm when each individual has the feeling of going beyond him- or herself and of accomplishing sensational things. This is because the basic affect in the case of love is happiness. Everyone is well aware that to show happiness is to show love. One can't see how happiness can be shown otherwise. But this affect is the product of a labour that it accompanies and guides, and which includes a lot of other aspects. Why? Because it is the experimentation of difference, the experimentation of a world suspended, for each of the two, upon the fact of being two.

– You also state that love is the truth of a disjunction, a truth that is not, then, a totality or knowledge. Could you explain that to us? For example, by taking up your formula of 'the atom u', which can seem very surprising for those who don't understand that love can be formalized. Love generally appears to be quintessentially 'that which cannot be formalized'.

– Here, we find ourselves in the 'impasse of formalization', as Lacan put it! But we can present things very simply. The hypothesis according to which the inaugural event is an encounter only has sense if you presume there is a situation of disjunction prior to the encounter. For there to be an encounter, there has first to be separation, potentially in a radical sense: the two parties didn't know each other and were respectively unaware that the other existed. We can also think of the separation created by sexuation, or by social status, age, or nationality. Or again, simply by the fact that individuals infinitely differ from one another.

Let's simply suppose there to be a disjunction. Either, there is total disjunction and the encounter is, then, a sham: you become involved in sham loves, in illusions, and contractual negotiations over reciprocal interests. This is the theory of classical moralism, according to which love, outside of sexual pleasure, is nothing or mere social convention. Or, you can consider that there is fusion since you go from disjunction to unity. This is the romantic vision, according to which love is not at all the scene of the Two but the transcendence of the One, the capacity of two subjectivities to really identify with one another, to merge together. But you can pass through the middle, if I may put it this way. You can pass, to employ political metaphors, between the Right and the far Left. The Right views marriage as a convenient illusion, a social arrangement, whereas the far Left views love as a glorious, transcendent fusion that changes everything but leads to death. In this case, the disjunction has to remain but 'not wholly'. The ground on which this scene of the Two is created doesn't aspire to the abolition of this disjunction but nor does it aspire to its being maintained as it is.

– Is a single point between disjunction and fusion sufficient to engender love?

– If one wants, in any case, to resolve the problem I'm referring to, then there does, indeed, have to be a point of connection – a single point, perhaps. The encounter has to leave a trace. One can also say that the trace is revealed through the encounter: the disjunction is indeed a disjunction but there is a point of intersection, a point of tangency. If not, it's not clear what 'encounter' means. The encounter must at first rely on almost nothing, which is the perception of a point. There is a common point. The construction of the scene of the Two consists in the Two being seen afresh on the basis of this common point and not on the basis of pure disjunction. When you meet, only this point exists as yet. This is something that always fascinates me: that you engage in such an incredible adventure knowing so little – all you know is that there is 'something'.

In the formalization I've proposed, there is 'man' and 'woman', because what I'm working on in this instance is sexuated disjunction, and then there is a point 'u', u as in universal or as in *Un* [One]. After the encounter, it will always be a matter of presenting things that in some way dilate the point or that surround it. Of course, there are times when you contract back to this point, on the only thing that really existed at the start. I propose, as a result, to present love as moments of systole and diastole, which is to say of expansion and contraction. This is empirically observable: there are moments of dilation when a fragment of the world is appropriated by the two in a truly dual fashion, and other moments when narcissism demands its rights and you fall back on the base, on something very close to the initial point. This play can lead to a moment when the *u* gives way and the topic of separation is opened up. In *In Praise of Love*,[2] I propose that one of the possible ways of defining love is as an obstinate struggle against separation. Every love stems from separation, with this thereby haunting, constantly and in spite of everything, the process.

Fidelity, love and desire, love and family

– Let's speak about 'fidelity'. Is the engagement that is fidelity essential to love or simply incidental?

– The common meaning of this term, especially when it's a question of love, is mainly negative: being faithful consists in not sleeping with someone else. When the word is pronounced in this context, this is clearly what one has in mind.

We touch here on a real and rather complicated question, which is that of the exact relations between desire and love. This question is raised, moreover, under many other forms than that of whether to sleep with someone or not. It is raised intrinsically because love has absolutely to incorporate desire. This is what distinguishes love from friendship or fondness. The body itself has to constitute a proof of love; it is engaged as a proof of love. Poor Auguste Comte, when he was wooing Clotilde de Vaux, never ceased asking her for what he called 'the indisputable proof', which she didn't want to give him! He wasn't wrong to speak of 'indisputable proof'. In sexual abandonment and in denudation before the other, there is an element of proof that attests that the body, our unique reality, is well and truly taken up in the scene of the Two: it's the

[2] Badiou, Alain, with Nicholas Truong, *In Praise of Love*, trans. Peter Bush, London, Serpent's Tail, 2012. Originally published as: *Eloge de l'amour*, Paris, Flammarion, 2009.

proof that the body doesn't remain set aside. Love has to incorporate desire. But desire itself is never, on the other hand, immediately connected to love; it has its own laws, which are not immediately those of love. It is one of the numerous heterogeneous things that love must be capable of integrating. It is not, then, without reason that fidelity can basically be said to be a very simple and observable modality of the discipline imposed upon desire by love.

– Fidelity is also an essential concept in your thought. What relation is there between the common meaning of the term you've just mentioned and the conceptual sense you give to the word 'fidelity'?

– I use the term 'fidelity' in a philosophical sense, which is one that applies to every truth procedure. This philosophical sense recalls that the origin of a truth procedure is an event. If I claim – as an individual, a body, and an element of the situation – to be within the truth procedure inaugurated by that event, I have to assume the consequences as tenaciously as possible: those of the event, of its nomination and of the engagement I've taken. In the case of love, it's a matter not only of the consequences of the encounter but also of the declaration. I've said 'I love you.' This has consequences. These are the consequences of an experimentation of the world by two. I need to show the required tenacity on this point because the thing doesn't keep going automatically. The consequences need to be unfolded and don't unfold all by themselves. Fidelity consists in being in the subjective element of these consequences. This means, basically, that one accepts to participate in the new subject made possible by the event.

– Fidelity is then always fidelity to an event, to the birth of a subject (here, a subject composed of two), which is to say that it is, ultimately, fidelity to a truth?

– I do, in fact, associate every truth procedure with a subject that consists, precisely, of this new orientation of experience rendered possible by an inaugural event. Instead of being completely centred on me, this new orientation of experience is partially decentred. I can no longer claim to be its centre. It's necessary to be faithful to this decentring. This fidelity designates a kind of norm that I impose upon myself, one which consists in not abandoning this decentring, or this new subject, for reasons strictly related to my fundamental narcissism or my irreducible singularity. In love, there is always, then, an element of discipline, which intersects with the trivial meaning, if I can put it this way, of the word 'fidelity'. I have to try to go on organizing my experience in a way that is incorporated to something that is not fully measured by it alone: which is to say that I am not the sole measure of a love. This is why love cannot be reduced to the lovers' psychology. Such a reduction presumes that the lovers' psychology would be love's measure. But love is a subject that is somewhat beyond psychology. Whence the necessity to be faithful to it, and all the more so in that it traverses storms, temptations and separations. Putting an end to a love is always disastrous. Even if you can accept, even desire, this disaster, the rupture remains, nonetheless, intrinsically disastrous.

– But doesn't the family, for its part, need to be reinvented? What meaning do you give to the family in the amorous procedure?

– I think that, in respect of love, the family stands in exactly the same relation as the State in respect of politics. In *The Origin of the Family, Private Property and the State*, Engels linked, very legitimately moreover, these three terms: the family, private property and the State. The family is supposed to be the socialized product of love, just as the State is supposed to be the product of politics. Except the State doesn't really need politics. I have even maintained that the State is, essentially, always depoliticized. It is a managerial instance; it doesn't put principles to work. In the same way, the family, as everyone knows, can very well exist without love.

The interrelation between the family and love poses, then, the same problems as the interrelation between the State and politics. Under the present conditions, no politics can act as though there wasn't the State and no love can act as though there wasn't the family. Simply, in both cases, the truth procedure is secretly subordinated to something other than itself. The State is a separate principle of authority, intended to assure the continuation and the reproduction of the collectivity, in the same way as the family is intended, in the last resort, to assure the continuation of the species. The finalities of the State and the family are not, as a result, of the order of principle or of truth, contrary to the finalities of politics and love.

– Love could, then, 'exceed' the family? Even do without it?

– Let's start by noting that we have, at the level both of the State and the family, a very singular pretension: two distinct finalities – one in terms of the Idea, truth and principles; the other in terms of 'persevering in being' as Spinoza would say – claim to be interconnected. The prevailing ideologies claim that the finality of the family is that of love and that the finality of the State is that of politics. This is in no way the case, but nor can these two finalities be said to function in a total disjunction. We are in a really complex situation. Further, as regards the State, Marx named this situation the 'withering away of the State'. Ideally, politics should organize the 'withering away of the State'; it is, therefore, completely in relation with the State but in such a way that it aims at its abolition. Similarly, love should ideally organize the withering away of the family.

I think that assigning the family as love's obligatory finality creates considerable difficulties for love. In the same way, making the takeover of State power the inevitable objective of politics creates considerable difficulties for politics. We're dealing, in fact, with figures of alienation, to use this terminology. Of course, the reproduction of the species has to be organized in some way or other. I am not going to embrace, in the name of love, a reproductive nihilism and exclaim: Let's abolish the species and everything will be alright! That would smack far too much of Schopenhauer!

– Would love, then, in relation to the family, have a political force?

– In fact, I retain something of the Marxian idea that is the most abandoned of all and also the strangest: even though politics is not going to make the State vanish as if by magic, it must nonetheless be co-extensive with the idea of a progressive withering away of the State and a substitution of its managerial figures with figures of association and creation. There where there is reproduction, there should be free association and creation. I think the same holds for the family. One of love's essential tasks is not at all, as people think, to construct a family but to invent forms that free the scene of the Two from family egoism. All this assumes, of course, the existence and love of children – for the family constructs a scene of the Two and brings children into the world but closes itself up within a collective narcissism. What seals all that is obviously inheritance. Everything ends up, therefore, being interrelated: the management of goods, the State and the family. The family becomes, as a result, what the contemporary world fundamentally wants it to be – a consumption unit. The family plays a formidable role in organizing consumption; it's a mercantile engorgement!

Love and philosophy, love and friendship

– According to its etymology, philosophy is 'the love of wisdom'. The verb *philein* (to love, to desire) plays, moreover, an important part in the definition of Platonic philosophy. Yet 'Eros' plays just as essential a role. In the *Symposium*, Socrates is identified with Eros. Likewise, it's as someone in love with Alcibiades that Socrates seeks to convey to him the wisdom that will render him apt for politics. This place that love has in Platonic philosophy is somewhat troubling. How do you interpret it?

– I'd add to your references that rather strange passage of the *Republic* where Socrates seeks to define the philosopher who will be attributed political power. All of a sudden, he states that in love you cannot love in a piecemeal manner but must love all of the loved being; you cannot, as it were, choose bits. To my mind, that amounts to opposing love and desire since desire desires partial objects, as Lacan would put it. Love, for its part, takes the being as a whole. This will lead Socrates to affirm that philosophy must take wisdom itself as a whole. We have then, in fact, this striking link between philosophy and what Plato calls love, with, into the bargain, as you've just recalled, that somewhat vacillating definition of philosophy as 'love of wisdom', 'friendship' or 'love' of wisdom: '*philein*'!

I think that this Platonic problem of the relation of love to philosophy can be analysed in two ways. The first consists in showing that love is a striking example of a capacity to pass from the sensible to something that is vaster and more essential. I'm not saying that it is expressly a question of the passage from the sensible to the intelligible, for that would be to fall into a sort of textbook Platonism. Yet what does Plato mean when he

declares, in the *Symposium*, that we are already on the
way to contemplating the Idea of the beautiful when we
contemplate a beautiful body? (On condition, of course,
that we love this beautiful body!) He wants to say that
love is what opens a singularity (a beautiful body) to
more than itself, to the Idea of the beautiful. The Idea
of the beautiful is in the beautiful body and, at the same
time, it is more than it – this being what Plato names
'participation'. The beautiful body participates in the
Idea of the beautiful but the Idea of the beautiful exceeds,
in a certain way, the beautiful body. Love as an effective
force always sees in the other something more than its
simple objective existence.

– You share this approach to love. Love has the capacity
to convey us beyond being – and, first of all, beyond the
being that we are ourselves.

– Yes, this extremely strong idea is one that I take up
in my own right. I think that love is an essential experience for philosophy. It is an existential practice that
attributes to the experience of the world something
more than my own finitude. Philosophy's relation to
love is a relation to one of the rare human experiences
that set up an excess in respect of oneself. This idea
is one that the modern world doesn't acknowledge.
Love is considered as a dependency, as something
that threatens my freedom and places me in a situation
in which I don't have control over myself. All of the
latter, which contemporary pragmatism considers to
be disastrous, are judged by Plato – and I follow him
here – as eminently positive. At last, there is a breach-
ing of the principle of interest as an animal principle!
Love surmounts the human animal principle all while
being propped upon it. It doesn't do this at the level
of great ideals but at a level both much closer to animality itself and, in a certain way, much more familiar
to everyone.

– But with Plato, at least as regards the figure of Socrates, love also seems to have an essential role in philosophy's transmission.

– This is the other analysis I spoke of a moment ago. How is philosophy transmitted? Its mode of transmission cannot be exclusively discursive and intellectual. It's an idea of this kind that we find in Plato. There is something about philosophy that requires the relation to the other to take on an amorous figure, at least metaphorically. In any case, this figure is not limited to the objectivity of what the other says, to her or his argumentation, but involves an amorous dimension that takes the other into account in a way that goes beyond me myself. Lacan and psychoanalysts analyse this as a transference love. The argument comes down to stating that there is no complete philosophical communication without transferential figures that are related to love for the person who is speaking. Philosophy would be singled out among all the disciplines by the characteristic of only being capable of completely assuming its function of transmission with the aid of transferential love. This explains, in particular, why the true philosophical scene in Plato is oral and not written. The body of the other has to be there, his or her voice has to resound.

To sum up, I follow Plato on these two points. I think that philosophy requires the experience of love, as the primitive, or proto-, experience of an opening-up of finitude, of the passage from the one to the two. This passage from one to two is the first opening-up of finitude – the smallest but, undoubtedly, also the most radical. Moreover, from the point of view of philosophical transmission's overall configuration, there is a particular function of transference. Why, for that matter? Because philosophy is not a discipline in the ordinary sense of the word. It entails knowledge but cannot be reduced to a form of knowledge. It cannot, then, be transmitted simply as a form of knowledge. It is the specific mode by which the Idea can govern subjectivity. It is the relation of subjectivity and the Idea, and such a relation cannot be reduced to knowledge.

– We've recalled that there is a certain ambiguity with respect to philosophy's etymology as either love or friendship. This implicitly raises the problem of the difference between love and friendship. But what, ultimately, is this difference? Is it enough to look for it in desire and sexuality?

– There is perhaps some degree of desire in friendship. We don't really know anything about it, after all. What's important is that, in love, desire has to be avowed and put into effect. The body's presence, its being offered up and exposed, attest to the character of love, to its holistic character. To speak like Lacan, love involves the being of the other and not such or such a trait, or such or such a partial object. From this perspective, sexuality has a particular function in love. It functions as a proof of total exposition, of total abandonment. It attests that there are no spaces off-limit in being-two, that nothing is withheld. The body is love's surface of exposition. Nudity is essential. It attests that nothing is set aside. Everyone knows that desire exists under other forms than an amorous one, yet it has to be taken up, as proof, within the discipline of love. Friendship accepts that a great deal of things remain in the background or set aside. This is also its charm. Friendship can be very intense but, nonetheless, have determined its bearings and what leeway it allows. Further, there are things you can bring into play in a friendship on the basis that they don't directly impinge upon it. As a result, you're able to discuss calmly what is happening to one or the other of you in a confidential and supportive way. A friend is someone to whom you talk about your loves precisely because you aren't in love with them.

– A friendship also begins, for its part, by an encounter, a coincidence. . . . Isn't there an amicable event?

– In my opinion, no. There is, obviously, an encounter. Yet the encounter doesn't function like an origin in friendship. Friendship is something that is both more comprehensive and more vague than love, more social-ized as well. You cannot, for all that, conclude there is a radical disjunction. A great many components of friendship are integrated into love. The reverse isn't true however: almost everything in friendship is found in love but love is far from being entirely encompassed by friendship. It's in this constitutive dissymmetry that you can single out friendship and love. Friendship, because it comprises a lot of zones that have been set aside, is in many respects a cautious relationship – not in a cal-culating sense but in the sense that you instinctively know what things you can talk about calmly and what things aren't worth mentioning. This organization and this caution mean that friendship can integrate very dif-ferent personalities. This is something that I'm very struck by: that you can have for friends people who are, in the end, very different from you. You couldn't live with them and love them in an amorous way. These differences of perspective and taste, of political views and rhythms of everyday life would end up impeding the ongoing construction of a scene of the Two but don't prevent amicable discontinuity.

It's for this reason that I think that the mode of relat-ing with friends is intrinsically episodic. Even if you see them often, it remains essentially episodic. A friend is not someone you're going to live with day-in, day-out, and speak to about everything. He or she is someone that you see with pleasure from time to time, and the fact of its being spread out like this forms part of what I call amicable caution. But the type of things making up the friendship you have, can, by and large, be identi-fied, with both of you agreeing. Lots of other things are excluded. That's why friendship is easily of an intellectual nature. You have intellectual friends. Yet you also have friends for going hunting or having a drink with.

– I would now like to take up the question of love more broadly and consider the question of alterity. In your work you approach the question of alterity through politics or love. Moreover, ethics is not for you a condition, unlike politics, love, art and science. The other is not, for you, inaccessible by essence or a moral transcendence; nor is the other a world or an atmosphere. How, then, does your work consider the question of the Other? Is alterity really able to be thought from the angle of love and politics alone? Isn't something lacking?

– A main characteristic of my philosophy is that it doesn't see 'the other' as a problem. Alterity is what there is. Everything is different from everything else, everything is other than everything else. Given that I am in an ontology that is radically an ontology of the multiple, difference or alterity is what I set out from: it's the regime of being. In a sense, alterity is not my problem. The question of relation is different: that there is alterity doesn't mean there is a relation between the various terms. I would even state that my ontology is primarily an ontology of alterity without relation. There aren't, then, relations at the level of being.

I only introduce relations at the level of appearing; it's a category pertaining to world and not to being. On this basis, that which interests me is not alterity as such. What meaning is to be given to the fact that two different terms are in a situation that is the same and that they share something? That's what interests me – the in-common. How is it that two ontologically distinct terms, totally immersed in the element of alterity that is the anarchy of being, can nonetheless have something in common?

– To have something in common is also to start to communicate, isn't it? How far can this communication go?

– In fact, the thesis I uphold more and more – which is a perfectly Platonic one, actually – concerns the conditions under which two subjects or two individuals really communicate. That two individuals really communicate means that they are effectively, and in a manner that can be made explicit, in relation with each other; they are not merely in the mechanical relations of exteriority normal in any situation whatsoever (given that everything is made up of unconnected multiplicities). I believe I've introduced in this respect a fairly radical thesis that sets down that the only veritable communication is communication marked by the Idea. Human animals are in communication only insofar as each of them is incorporated within a truth procedure. Communication is as exceptional a phenomenon as truths are. When things aren't of this exceptional order, there isn't really communication but merely a rudimentary relation that is normed by the survival of one and all in a universe constituted by the appearances of indifferent ones.

I think, then, that an individual effectively interiorizes the necessity of the other when both individuals co-belong to the same subject, to the same subject of truth. Love is the first experience of this type. There is real sharing, real communication, between the individuals incorporated within the amorous procedure, even if communication in this instance must not be understood as something rational or easy. It is itself part of the labour of love.

Generally, such sharing or communication between human individuals enveloped or enfolded within a truth procedure is, in its effective existence, a singular experience. There isn't, as a result, any general theory of alterity in this sense; any theory of the figures in which communication marked by an Idea occurs is always singular, on a case-by-case basis, since only when marked by the Idea is there communication. 'Communism', for example, is a word that expresses the common, the in-common. But it doesn't refer to an ontology of the in-common; it refers to the necessity of working to extend the exceptional character of truth procedures within which communication is effective.

Under these conditions, some simple examples of communication include not only two people engaged in a love procedure, of course, but also a group of people involved in a real and in-depth discussion of a mathematical problem, a theatre public, participants in a political demonstration or two people looking at the same painting.

– This allows us to speak of the 'subject'. You take this concept in what seems a very particular sense – one that isn't, in any case, that of the individuality of mind. Could you specify what you understand by 'subject'?

– To clarify this point, let's start with love and then generalize. Let's suppose that we experience a great love. Then, let's ask ourselves what the subject of this love is. The first way of answering this would be to say that there are two: i.e., the two individuals in love. The other would be to say that there isn't one. I maintain, rather, that there really is construction of a subject because there is an experience, the experience of the two, that is shared vis-à-vis the world. There is, then, a subject of love that doesn't let itself be reduced to the pure and simple addition or aggregation of two individuals. Now, let's generalize from this. Under the contingent conditions of an event – an insurrection, for example – a process, a truth procedure, is set in motion.

The individuals who are incorporated within this procedure are, then, all going to constitute a subject together. A subject can take various forms. In the twentieth century, the party, class, the proletariat were conceived as subjects. In all these cases, it is evident that 'subject' designates something that emerges with a truth procedure, something that is the orientation of this procedure. It's not a matter of individuals as such.

I've proposed to systematize this by showing that every truth procedure, insofar as it has an orientation and resolves problems, can be considered a subject. Whence the term 'a subject of truth'. Say, you go to an art exhibition and you find yourself dazzled by a painting; this involves your incorporation within a truth procedure – in this specific case, an artistic one. This happens frequently, even if, from a certain point of view, works of art are rare. The experience of incorporation, for its part, is frequent. What's involved is an experience of subjectivization: the human individual, in his/her absolute singularity and as an element of the world, becomes a part of this body of truth that appears. The work of art being contemplated is the symbol or manifestation of this appearance of a body of truth.

– You even maintain that the subject experiences, as a result, a certain immortality.

– Indeed. I maintain that the subject experiences a kind of immortality when it participates in one way or another in something that is of the order of truth. This constitutes a huge difference with the individual, who is, unquestionably, not immortal! With incorporation, there appears a kind of immortality that is potential but, nonetheless, effective since truth procedures, in their products or results, are eternally available. And I do mean available – available for a procedure of subjectivization.

The positions man/woman; love and sexuality

– For you, the difference between masculine and feminine really has a meaning: there is a masculine position and a feminine position. You speak of 'imperative' and 'immobility' for the position 'man' and of 'wandering' and 'narrative' for the position 'woman'. In the context of a conflict, you describe the man as mute and violent and the woman as garrulous and full of demands. Masculine and feminine really do, then, exist?

– I think that it's within the very terms of the amorous procedure that masculine and feminine find their definition. Love is what creates the sexes, it's what reveals them. Of course, like everyone else, I know there is a biological sexual differentiation, yet, if one's interested in the question of truths, it becomes clear that a position 'man' and a position 'woman' are constructed within love itself. The positions 'man' and 'woman', viewed from within love, are then generic: they have nothing to do with the empirical sex of the people engaged in the love relation. I fully recognize that there can be homosexual love. The words 'man' and 'woman' relate, for me, uniquely to positions that are internal to the amorous procedure. Moreover, the play of these positions is, I believe, universal. In the amorous procedure, the positions are potentially open to change; they are not irreversibly assigned to one or the other party. Depending on the circumstances, one can be more feminine in arguments while the other is more masculine in times of peace. But it remains possible to formally define each person's position.

Formally, this position is defined by a polarity: namely, separation and the struggle against separation. If there wasn't separation, there wouldn't be permanent struggle against separation. But the converse is true: if there wasn't this struggle against separation, there wouldn't be separation. Two positions are defined by this polarity. For the masculine position, if there is struggle against separation there must be separation. The feminine position focuses rather on the struggle against separation: certainly, there is separation but the struggle against separation is first necessary. This is why the man is always viewed by the woman as someone who is going to leave or who is in the process of leaving. Literature is full of this polarity. Of course, this doesn't mean that love doesn't exist. It means that love constantly recalls the existence of this internal polarity of separation, which doesn't prevent it from struggling against it in its own way. Love recalls incessantly the existence of that against which it struggles. This is touched upon magnificently in Beckett's *Enough*, where the woman ends up declaring she left the man because this was, ultimately, what he desired. This paradox, in all its splendour, is internal to love.

We have, therefore, a dialectization of separation and non-separation. There is something in masculinity that sees non-separation from the point of view of separation while something in femininity sees separation from the point of view of non-separation. It can be shown that these respective positions of man and woman are coherent. They are immanent to love, without their relation to empirical sex being easy to stabilize, other than in statistical, random ways. All that can be said is that the masculine position is fairly often occupied by men. This fact isn't, however, of much interest to philosophers – but rather sociologists!

– You state in this respect that the position 'man' is defined as follows: 'What will have been true is that we were two and not at all one.' As for the position 'woman', this is defined by: 'What will have been true is that two we were and that otherwise we were not.'[3]

---

[3] 'What is Love?', in *Conditions* [1992], trans. Steven Corcoran, London, Continuum, 2008, p. 194.

– That's more or less what I've just said, isn't it? It's nevertheless better expressed in those terms, even if it's a bit condensed!

– Is the importance of these two terms for you what prompts you to declare that love is heterosexual in principle?

– By stating that love is heterosexual, I want to underline that two distinct positions are always to be found within love itself, and this is the case regardless of the empirical sex of the partners. These two distinct positions introduce a structuration of the scene of the Two. They take the two not only as a numerical two but as a heterogeneous two. Of course, we have a numerical two here, but this is also a qualitative two. Once again, I absolutely recognize the fact that there are homosexual loves. I've known some that were very long-lasting, very passionate. Yet, this doesn't constitute an objection since there are always two identifiably distinct positions in homosexual relations. Everyone will agree to speak here of a position 'man' and a position 'woman'. These could just as well be called something else, but that's not the problem.

When I say 'heterosexual', I want in any case to insist on *heteros*. There is something of the other in this affair, of the sexuated other. I won't go so far as to borrow Lacan's famous formula, 'I name heterosexual whosoever loves women', which amounts to classing all lesbians as heterosexuals! At the same time, I clearly see how to understand it. Were we to take a complete phenomenology of sexuated positions, we would see that the feminine position holds the view of the love relationship that can most readily be expressed in terms of *heteros*, which is to say: 'We were two, otherwise we were not.' It's the *heteros* that is crucial here.

– Finally, a parable will serve as a conclusion: 'Love passes through desire like a camel through the eye of a needle.'[4]

– I'd readily take up the formula of Lacan: 'Love is the approach of being.' It's the totality of the other that's in question. As such, it consists in dealing with a hotch-potch of immense alterities. Certainly, you try to control these alterities in constructing a common world. It nevertheless remains the case that in love, without altogether realizing it at the start, you are dealing with an infinity. The progressive discovery of different strata of this infinity is, moreover, one of the problems, but also one of the joys, of amorous construction.

In desire, on the other hand, it is always a question of the desire of an object. I agree with Lacan on this point: the object of desire is a partial object, even if this partial object is lodged somewhere in the body of another. There is an intrinsic finitude of desire, due to its cause always being an object, whereas it is not an object that is the cause of love, but a being. And from the point of view of love, there is something narrow about desire. This is why I state that love has to pass through the eye of the needle of desire. It has to pass through this. Sublimated love, platonic love, doesn't hold up. Everyone knows that love has to pass through desire. It's necessary to get the immensity proper to love to pass through something that is very fixed, very narrow.

The magnificence of amorous sexuality, when it exists, but also the figures of its failure, are due to the fact that the amorous assertion is in disprepostion with the active sexuality. The problem will consist in constructing a sexuality such that this disproportion is attenuated. Duration, the invention by love of a

---

[4] Ibid., p. 190. (Translation modified.)

sexuality appropriate to the enchanted world of the Two, will remedy as much as possible this disproportion. Except if the standard family model is adopted, in which conjugal sexuality is limited to making babies. But this is suffocation by the State! And in that case it is certain that love fails itself.

The amorous experience is, when all is said and done, a good means of comparing what being and object, the infinite and finitude, are. It is not a matter of comparing them in isolation from one another but in their possible combination. It's necessary that love, in its constitutive procedure, passes through something that is of a different order than itself.

3

Art

The singularity of the artistic condition

– Art is, for you, one of philosophy's four conditions. In what way does this condition particularly question philosophical thought?

– As regards what's specific about the artistic condition, I first have to bring up a point that already shows the singularity of philosophy's relation to art. The world of art is a powerful example of the presence of multiplicity in truths. Artistic multiplicity contrasts not only with the, all in all, relatively rare character of great political sequences (those that serve to create truths) but, equally, the quasi-omnipresence of the amorous procedure. The relation between art and the arts is, moreover, a thoroughly classic problem in philosophy. What exactly is the principle that music, painting and sculpture have in common? This is a question that has tormented philosophers for a very long time. Generally, it takes the traditional form of how to classify the arts, their possible hierarchy. Is there an art that recapitulates all the others, a supreme art?

These questions interest me for reasons that are, in a certain sense, ontological since they come up in the relation between: multiplicity, which is a fundamental ontological term; event, a term relating, on the contrary, to pure singularity; and truths, which are, at once, plural and each of them absolutely singular. Art raises these resolutely specific questions because of its strange multiplicity, the basis of which is fairly difficult to elucidate. It is hardly satisfactory to link this to the multiplicity of the senses. In fact, none of the classificatory principles totally accounts for it.

A second point consists in noting that the question of the relation between being and appearing lies at the very core of art. Artistic effect is wholly within the sensory sphere: it's what is seen, what is heard. We're in the order of appearing, of that which appears. Yet, we have the feeling that something essential, something slightly veiled, is present. If I draw on my jargon, I'd speak of the relation between ontology and logic. This question has, in any case, posed a problem to philosophy since its origin. Plato's suspicion of imitative arts is, in this respect, simply an aspect of his suspicion of appearance. For Hegel, on the other hand, art is the sensible form of the Idea, which is a typical dialectical example of the possibility of the quasi-charnel presence of the absolute Idea itself.

– But isn't art always embedded in specific cultures? Philosophy, for its part, never loses sight of the universal.

– The third reason art interests philosophy (particularly mine, in this case) concerns the relation to the universal. This is an extremely complicated issue. Of the different procedures, art is certainly the most implicated in the diversity of cultures, languages and historicities. A poem is rendered in a particular language. Art is, moreover, mixed up with religion and its histories, with cultural singularities. Are there indigenous or primitive arts? Is there only one history of art or are there several? Are Western art and Chinese art really related? These questions pertain to art's relation to anthropology, cultures, and human singularities. It becomes complicated, as a result, to determine where its universality takes root.

To sum up, I'd say that art questions the concepts of philosophy on three levels. First, that of multiplicity: there are arts, in a particularly striking manner. Second, the relation between being and appearing: art is the form of truth that is the most implicated in the sensory realm. Finally, the question of the relations between universality and relativity. Given art's irreducible cultural multiplicity, it is often presented today as a challenge to universality. Is there a 'great Art' opposed to popular arts? This is something that henceforth seems difficult to decide. It's what explains that art is one of the roots of contemporary relativism.

The event and the artistic subject

– We know that everything begins for you with an event. What is, then, an artistic event?

– Artistic events are great mutations that almost always bear on the question of what counts, or doesn't count, as form. The history of art, particularly the history of Western art, is the history of the progressive incorporation within the domain of form of things that were, up until then, considered as unformed, deformed, or foreign to the world of form. The shifts towards abstraction in painting or towards modifications of tonality in music are cases in point. An artistic event is always the accession to form, or the formal promotion of a domain that had been considered extraneous to art. There really is creation of a formal domain that was unperceived or denied up until then. I'm struck by the fact that the expansion of formal resources constitutes the core of great artistic events, whether it's a matter of the invention of atonal music by Schoenberg, the advent of the possibility of a non-figurative painting, or – and nonetheless – the advent, with Haydn and Mozart, of classical music in its tonal figure, which was to dominate the entire eighteenth century. The artistic event is signalled by the advent of new forms.

– Fine. But what, then, is an artistic subject? Is it the innovatory artist, who's capable of creating an event?

– This is a more delicate question. Traditionally, the subject is considered to be the creator. This is the figure of the Artist, a figure that reaches its height in Romanticism. It is striking to see that in the eighteenth century musicians were still artisans, almost craft workers. There was even a semi-collective side to creation. Someone like Bach depicts himself not as a genial artist in the nineteenth-century sense but rather as a conscientious artisan. The advent of an artistic subject is partially co-extensive with nascent romanticism. Its first canonical figures are Beethoven and Schumann. The arrival of more solitary figures is palpable in music and painting alike.

I'm proposing a total upheaval of this point of view. In reality, the artist is only a subject in a thoroughly empirical sense, in the sense that s/he is the producer of the work. What's interesting, however, is to determine where the subject is in the work – and not at its source or origin. I propose thinking of the subject constituted in art by the artistic event as consisting precisely of the system of works. The artistic subject is constituted by works or by groups of works. Take, for example, the musical upheaval at the turn of the twentieth century. What constitutes a subject, what transforms the musical subjectivity of the listener, is a system of works. I've proposed the term 'configuration' to designate the fact that works – not a single work, but a system – configure a new subjectivity.

This entails, as a result, a protocol of incorporation (as for all the other – scientific, political or amorous – types of subjects:): those who listen to the work, or attempt to listen to it, will have to transform their individuality, their relation to art and their particular way of listening. Incorporation within a subjectivity consists in this transformation. The subject creates, therefore, new listeners, or rather a new listener, and not simply new creators or new artists. The difficulty of this incorporation is, furthermore, one of the problems of contemporary music. Yet this difficulty already existed at other periods. This was clearly the case for symbolist or Mallarmean poetry, in which we can see a rupture vis-à-vis the reader of the poetry of Victor Hugo. The period was aware of this, moreover. It's still the case today that we know listeners of contemporary music to be relatively rare: this music's creation of its listeners takes time.

– Event, subject . . . But where, then, is artistic truth found? In what way is art capable of truth?

– Truth is here the generic set of the evental consequences of these mutations of art. It's a sequence of a specific art. There is, for example, a truth of the resources of sound discovered by serial music. What's interesting, and what appears to be more discernible in art than in the other conditions, is that the evental mutation renders the truth of the sequence that precedes it. It is absolutely evident, for example, that Schoenberg's atonal proposition yields the truth of the point reached by tonality itself. In reality, Schoenberg produces, in a certain sense, the truth of Wagner or Mahler. The latter appear as figures of tonality's decomposition at a juncture where tonality could no longer continue as such. This impossibility of continuing is sealed or validated by the new musical creation. The event opens up in this way the possibility of understanding the very situation in which it is produced. Dodecaphonic, then serial, music produces a definitive truth of the whole tonal sequence at the same time as it puts an end to it.

This phenomenon – these retroactive mechanisms – is particularly illuminating in respect of art. Basically, it's because contemporary music exists that we really know what the tonal ground of classical and romantic music was. Similarly, what pictorial representation consists in became known once non-figurative painting was accepted. Look at paintings from 1912 to 1913, the period of Picasso and Braque – the grand cubism. The relation that they have to representation isn't abolished – one still makes out guitars, tobacco packets and so on – but it's brought to a close, which isn't the same thing; we're no longer dealing with imitation but with reconstruction. This reconstruction of the visible is wrought through geometrical forms and arrangements in space that aren't arrangements of perspective. At the same time as it brings the previous system of representation to an end, it indicates in what this consisted. That a truth is the truth of the situation in which it occurs while pronouncing at the same time the rupture with the latter, is a lesson that art imparts better than the other procedures – even if this is also seen in certain aspects of science.

– The creator and the spectator are, then, merely incorporated within a subject that is impersonal, even though it's singular; they are incorporated within a set of works oriented by something new that suddenly surges forth, an event?

– Yes, absolutely.

– This notion is fairly hard to grasp, I feel, at least if one identifies 'subject' with 'person' – which is what we normally tend to do. Can you be more precise on this point?

– In reality, the creator is absent from this affair that is the work. The creator is not the centre of gravity. I am interested, then, in the work, on the one hand, and in the listener or the spectator, on the other. I'm Mallarmean on this point: the creator is a vanishing cause. Of course, s/he is a cause because s/he is included in the work but a vanishing cause. There is never anything to be gleaned from the creator. Scrutinizing the soul of the creator in order to discover something or other about the work has never yielded anything whatsoever.

– You would, then, agree on this point with Deleuze, who persistently criticized those seeking the secret of the work of art in the artist's personality?

– Absolutely – and with many others. It's a contemporary idea. In the end, there is a sort of anonymity of the work, or a vanishing of the creator in the work. As Mallarmé put it: 'The Master is absent.' He has 'gone to draw tears from the Styx . . . '

– 'With this sole object honoured by Nothingness.'[1]

– And precisely, the sole object honoured by Nothingness is the poem itself.

– Nevertheless the resonance of the name is very strong for most people. Many will find it hard to admit that

---

[1] These lines come from Mallarmé's 1887 untitled sonnet, often referred to as the 'Sonnet in X', which begins: *Ses purs ongles très haut dédiant leur onyx* (Her pure nails held high dedicating their onyx). [Translator's note]

when they're exposed to a piece of music, they are exposed to an anonymous sequence of art. They will say: that's Mozart or that's Beethoven. They will come to love a piece of music because it's Mozart or Beethoven.

– I'd readily take up a political analogy to clarify this point. In the Leninist or Bolshevik period, the political subject was the party. Now, what is the party? It's what orients the political process. The party is nothing other than all the actions it undertakes, that it sets in motion. If you try to reduce it to a formalism, you reduce it to its leader. This is what happened. The party was said to be Stalin, just as, moreover, dodeca-phonic music was said to be Schoenberg. The proper name intervenes here as a substitute: it testifies to the fact that one doesn't exactly know what can be said about the subject. For the subject is the process of the works themselves. This is particularly clear in art and constitutes a great part of its interest.

Just as there was a cult of the personality in politics, so there was a cult of the creator, which moreover paved the way for the political cult of personality. Stalin was viewed, fundamentally, as a Beethoven or Mozart of politics. This fetishization of the creator is totally sterile and serves as a substitute for an in-depth comprehension of what is taking place. If you eliminate all fetishization, you find yourself disarmed before an artistic sequence and the question is raised of how this transforms individuals through incorporation.

Artistic incorporation

– Precisely. I'd like you to clarify this incorporation a bit more. The subject in art is, then, impersonal. How is one incorporated in a process, within an impersonal procedure?

– What we have to understand is that works configure a new artistic sequence. In this configuration, a generic truth of the situation of a given art becomes progressively discernible. Individuals are incorporated within this truth by mutations in their way of relating to this art. These mutations affect the way the work is defined and how it is seen or heard. What is it to listen to music? What is it to view a painting? It's mutations of this order that interest me, mutations which the creator was, basically, the first to have been seized by.

– Artistic subjectivity amounts then to seeing or hearing something new?

– For me, subjectivity is signalled by the possibility of an Idea, of a new Idea – to use the terminology that is mine today, that of the third volume of *Being and Event* . . . which doesn't yet exist! In art, it's a matter of a new Idea of what a given art is: a new Idea of painting, of music. And incorporation always takes place by accepting this Idea. This personal acceptance and incorporation within the Idea are what makes it possible, via the connection to the Idea, to hear something that wasn't heard or to see something that wasn't seen. The subject, for its part, is the real of this Idea. In other words, what renders this Idea possible is the works' existence. The real of this Idea is, strictly speaking, the subject of this sequence, what orients it, what makes it exist, what causes it to be real.

– How is our epoch to be described from the point of view of art? On the one hand, there are those who promote a democratization of creation as though absolutely everyone is an artist, with this 'democratization' doing nothing but accentuate the artwork's mercantile character and augment the number of more or less questionable works. On the other hand, the more informed or exigent artistic spaces aren't conveying any clear image of what creation might be today.

– We're no longer dealing strictly with a philosophical question here but with issues of conjunctural analysis that aren't necessarily able to be settled! I'll nonetheless try, in spite of everything, to say a thing or two. What we're the contemporaries of is the petering out, in art but also in other domains, of the constellation of events that reoriented things at the beginning of the twentieth century. In the sequence spanning the end of the nineteenth century to the beginning of the twentieth, all the arts went through a period of re-foundation. The plastic arts declared that the figure of representation, imitative of the natural model, had come to an end. Music declared that the salience of tonality had come to an end. With the Bauhaus, architecture became a question of function, breaking with the neo-classical and ornamental vision that had dominated the field since the seventeenth century. Poetry, by introducing prose and putting an end to the alexandrine, broke with what seemed to be its age-old definition: that of embedding expression in collectively endorsed rhythmic codes.

As I put it in *The Century*,[2] what we experienced there was an extraordinary moment – one that should be placed alongside the great creative periods of the history of humanity: the fifth and fourth centuries BC in Greece and the fifteenth and sixteenth centuries in Europe. Over a span of several years, the creative capacity in all the domains seemed limitless, so to speak. Painting and music weren't the only ones concerned. It was the period of Einsteinian relativity, the creation of modern algebra, psychoanalysis, the rise of cinema. . . . It's stupefying. The First World War fell in the midst of this like a blade. It's to be noted that, in Greece, the

---

[2] *The Century*, trans. Alberto Toscano, Cambridge, Polity, 2007. Originally published as *Le Siècle*, Paris, Seuil, 2005.

Peloponnesian war also occurred right in the middle of
its creative efflorescence.

It is very striking to note that mutations on a scale
such as these, sweeping up the totality of the arts,
succeed one another for no more than some twenty odd
years. This gave rise to extremely violent phenomena.
Profound habits of incorporation – to take up the
vocabulary we used a minute ago – were suddenly
uprooted. Art was split in two, with flagrant ruptures
appearing between an avant-garde and the shreds
that remained, in spite of everything, of the old habits.
This period was a real earthquake in the artistic field.
I'd define the present conjuncture by the fact that the
last consequences of this earthquake still exist. My
feeling is, however, that the sequence it opened is in
the process of coming to an end. This is shown by
the repeated themes of 'the end of the avant-gardes',
'post-modernism' . . .

– 'Aesthetic relativism' . . . And 'deconstruction'?

– Numerous names can be given to the phenomenon
but these names all converge towards the idea that this
radical, avant-garde ambition of beginning something
else completely from scratch and radically negating
the past, which was the ambition of this great twentieth century, has exhausted its charms and virtues.
This great ambition worked with the idea that art was
in the period of its end, that a tabula rasa would be
made of the conceptions that had prevailed previously.
One was going to do something else. This idea of
tabula rasa was, moreover, parallel to the revolutionary
political idea in its most tightly drawn form.

– What can we expect, then, from art today and
tomorrow? Should we morosely resign ourselves to
accrediting the thesis of 'the end of art' – just as some
believe in 'the end of history' – or to some sort of eternal

return of the same possibilities of invention? Alternatively, should we give art a new project, and what should this be?

– We're in an artistic situation that's altogether confused and uncertain because we are in an interval period when art's forces will have to be reconstituted in an infinitely more affirmative modality – one that's infinitely more bound to real processes and political proposals. The most interesting experiments seem to me, in any case, those that don't want to continue with a generalized deconstruction of previous models or with attributing a special virtue to negation. These experiments attempt to catch hold of shreds of the real by the formal means available and to affirm, within the formal resource of art, something regarding the contemporary world. Cinema potentially offers some significant undertakings in this direction, just as do certain fragments of poetic creation that are not without interest. But nothing has been decided triumphally. There isn't any major orientation, which is why there is a proliferation of schools and experiments in a situation where anything is possible. But we well know that when anything's possible, nothing is.

This situation is, moreover, more general than a situation limited to art. It's an interval situation due to the crisis of the Idea. This is flagrant in politics, where the crisis of the communist Idea is the very crisis of the political idea as such. In art, the crisis of the Idea is made manifest by the twilight of that period when art was fuelled by a radical critical methodology. Art was criticism, particularly the criticism of art. I think that we have to go back into a period of criticism of criticism, into a period where art can rediscover an affirmative function.

– You don't judge our artistic period very positively, then?

– To be frank, I don't think we're in a major artistic period. I think we're in a period that is certainly interesting, with lots of ramifications and contrasting directions, but it's a period of research and obscurity, waiting for foundational events – which are, as always, unable to be calculated in advance. This is not without precedents. The mid eighteenth century, for example, before the creation of the classical style in music, before Haydn, before the reappearance of neo-classicism in painting: what we have at that time are the baroques in music, François Boucher in painting and the fêtes galantes – even if Watteau succeeded in doing something. It's obvious that the mid eighteenth century is a period when classical art strictly said is depleted and something new hasn't yet really emerged. In terms of its matrix, this something new was to be romanticism in poetry from Goethe on, the classical style in music and the novel in literature. I think we're in a period of this nature. As Ibsen said, 'the old beauty is no longer beautiful and the new truth is not yet true.'[3]

– We referred in our first interview to Lenin's idea that, in periods of political inactivity, art is a combination of mysticism and pornography. Would this be the case for us today?

– I think the formula can be taken up. We've probably a bit more pornography today than mysticism – though, then again, the phenomenon described as the 'return of religions' could be considered to participate in all this. The present politico-aesthetic situation lends itself, in fact, to the return of the religious, which is to say, to tradition, to the sinister invocation of tradition. We

---

[3] Badiou is quoting here from Ibsen's play *Emperor and Galilean*. The quotation is not, however, exact. What Ibsen actually writes is: 'the old beauty is no longer beautiful and the new truth is no longer true' (Act II). [Translator's note]

have to accord to Lenin that this is an aspect of transition periods with respect to politics, art and, finally, people's lives. When you have a crisis of the Idea, you get this sort of thing: the tension of ordinary human animals who, on the one hand, seek shelter in the most familiar sectors of their existence (the family, tradition) and, on the other, abandon themselves to nihilism and the most tempting figures of debauchery. If you don't live under the sign of a consistence of the Idea, of a minimal creation of sense through the incorporation of the human animal that you are within this Idea, then you will necessarily have this bipolarity: either you take shelter in animal tradition with its codes, or anything goes.

High art versus popular art

– I'd like to know how you set out the relation between high art and popular art. The expansion of popular art is one of the traits of our time, bringing with it the risk that the very existence of a high art comes to be forgotten. Many believe, for example, that 'contemporary music' is rock 'n' roll. My question is, however, at the same time a provocative one. It seems to me that your categories could be applied to a group like Metallica, who, in the early 1980s, got form to surge from the unformed by the fact that these musicians raised an unprecedented brutality and discordance to the level of a system. What more is there to be found in Boulez or Schoenberg?

– I claim that there is no kind of formal invention that can be pointed to in forms of popular music that hasn't been anticipated, usually well in advance, in serious music. If we want to hail the eruption of brutality in music, we should look towards Stravinsky and Varese. And even in certain aspects of Wagner. In reality, there is no such thing as popular art. The expression is meaningless. In what way does the adjective 'popular' specify or determine the word 'art'? This category has to be jettisoned. There is music, full-stop. Music will be judged on the basis of its capacity to deal with formal inventions. It will, then, become clear that the degree of complexity, of inventiveness, of so-called serious music is without any common measure with that said to be popular. It was necessary, moreover, to say 'serious' solely because there was music said to be popular. The latter should be called music of entertainment, which is in no way defamatory.

Of course, this music of entertainment comprises norms and hierarchies, based, moreover, on what this music borrows from serious music. Popular music is all the better for borrowing from the latter! The Beatles were innovatory, in terms of music of entertainment, only because they extensively plundered forms of serious music, going back to Bach. They introduced forms of orchestration and vocal inflexions that had already been introduced previously.

The sole exception, and this must be incorporated within the history of serious music, is jazz. With jazz, we're dealing with a sphere of formal propositions that serious music hadn't wholly anticipated, particularly because of the large-scale introduction of an element of improvisation. The latter was found in Eastern music but wasn't at all characteristic of Western music's genius. Don't forget either that 'popular' music has ripped off absolutely everything of jazz's style.

What's most striking is that jazz was, with an astounding rapidity, to progressively intersect with the most sophisticated problems of serious music. With Archie Shepp or Coltrane, we're in a sophistication, including on the level of improvisation, that is extremely close to the upheavals of tonality and the innovatory subtleties of contemporary music. The inventive forms of jazz and contemporary music can be seen to converge, with their being brought into an extremely narrow proximity. This is clearly discernible in the post-war period, in which jazz's trajectory, from Charlie Parker to its more recent forms, tangentially joins serious music.

– Is it possible to generalize? Is all art serious or attached to high art forms?

– Yes. What's true of jazz is true to a certain degree of all art. Design, for example, is linked to fine art, while banal architecture has its roots in inventions that go back to the 1920s or 1930s. I have a son who adores rap and who's very knowledgeable about its successive stages. I keep myself up to date, as a result! And I've been struck to see that the rappers whom you feel have a slightly poetico-rhythmical quality (since rap is poetico-rhythmical more than musical) are people who have encountered or come into contact with veritable art, either of a poetical vein or a musical one.

I'm proposing, therefore, the fairly radical move of suppressing the phrase 'popular art'. The idea of art's unity, the unity it has always had, has to be defended. There's no opposition to make between high art and popular art. Certainly, there's an art of entertainment, and there's no question of denying that this entails hierarchies. Yet these hierarchies are always linked, ultimately, to the becomings of real procedures of art, period.

– What would you reply to those who would object to you that popular art created new forms, innovatory forms, in the twentieth century? Isn't cinema altogether a form of popular art that hardly stems from a pre-existent high art? And what about artistic forms like graffiti or spray painting?

– I'd reply that cinema is, first of all, the invention of a technology. It was from the very development of this technology that something having a singular artistic value gradually came to stand out, all while remaining in the element of entertainment – as is always the case when a new technological or formal set-up appears. Look at the case of oil painting, for example. As for graffiti murals, these have, in fact, a great tradition behind them, and even a hidden tradition. In their best aspects – in particular, their spontaneity – they are direct descendants of the poster art of the 1920s; they're a creation of Russian modernism. Moreover, there are a great number of things in primitive Soviet iconography that could be found to announce graffiti. We could also refer to the magnificent mural paintings of the Mexican communist school, from the 1930s on. Ultimately, when an artistic form appears, its genealogy has to be looked for and this is always related to what can be called high art. In the art of entertainment, interesting works having value can be produced. Yet what they have of value is always a product of the history of truths, of the history of forms created in the element of art in the strict sense

– You are clearly interested in cinema. You appear, moreover, in a recent film by Jean-Luc Godard, in which play yourself.[4] I've heard it said that you would like to direct a film yourself. I'd like to ask you: what is the cinema, from a philosophical perspective?

– The broad, philosophical definition I propose is that cinema is an art in which the Idea's mode of presence

---

[4] The film in question is Godard's *Film Socialisme*, which premiered at the Cannes Film Festival in 2010. In the film's first part, set on a Mediterranean luxury cruise ship serving as an allegory of Europe, Badiou lectures on Husserl to an empty auditorium. [Translator's note]

is visitation. I understand by this a mode of presence that is neither incarnation, as can be found in the case of classical painting or sculpture, nor imitation, realization, and so on. Cinema is an art that uses movement. The modality of potential intensity and the figure of truth proper to this movement are always of a transitory nature. It's not a visitation in the same sense as music is, since music is constructed – elaborated down to the last detail – in order for the Idea to be set out in its temporal fluctuation. Cinema, on the other hand, is an absolutely impure art, an art that takes art's possible impurity to its extreme. It's got everything in it: music, theatre, actors, images, decors. It's a hotchpotch! It works with an infinity of parameters that are, as such, impossible to control, with this being more and more the case. In its black and white, and silent era, the cinema was much more controlled, and therefore more fully perfected, than it is today.

What cinema is, then, is the chance given, in this mobile impurity, to an intense visitation of the Idea – a visitation that is often fragmentary, that dissolves and reappears. It's also the charm of cinema that you never clearly know in advance what is going to happen. Even the film-maker doesn't really know this. Between the conditions of the film's making, with its elaborate machinery and continually repeated takes, and what the film is, there is a huge gap. The outcome is very much a matter of chance.

– Insofar as cinema is an art for the masses, is this incompatible with the creation of authentic cinematographic works of art?

– It is true that cinema is the great contemporary art for the masses. You will note that certain forms of poetry have functioned as forms of mass art at certain periods. This was the case in ancient Greece with the Homeric epopees, or even, no doubt, tragedy. Victor Hugo's poetry was an art for the masses in the nineteenth century. Today, when you want to name the indubitable works of art that are also artworks for the masses, it's the films of Chaplin that immediately come to mind. They are indubitable works of art in the sense that you find in them the visitation of an Idea in the impurity of cinematographic movement. Cinema is the art that, still today, seems to me the most alive, the most active. Even if it's affected by the uncertainty that has befallen all the other arts, it's nonetheless the least uncertain. It seems to me that it conquered this position at the end of the First World War and has, in fact, kept it right up until today. It's an art that has formally captured more important parts of the real – the real of the contemporary world – than the other arts. Were you to ask yourself, for example, what traces of May '68 there might be in art, you'd have to look for them in Godard. Nowadays, where are the artistic traces of the decomposition of the Soviet Union? In the Armenian and Kazak films, the films of the Soviet periphery, that have appeared since the end of the 1980s as thoroughly significant works of art. I'd say the same with respect to the appearance of a great Asian cinema. I'm not speaking about Japanese cinema, well known for a long time, but about a great Korean or Chinese cinema. In the realm of art, this cinema reflects and says something essential about the growing power and importance of these regions of the world.

Cinema has succeeded in retaining an affirmative element. The best proof of this is that the branch of cinema that played the critical game, the game of the avant-garde – 'experimental cinema' – never really took hold. Cinema is not defined from the strict point of view of experimental cinema, whatever might be the merits of the latter, for that matter. It has remained an art for the masses, creating great works in some cases, and hasn't disintegrated into the thematic of the critique of art and the dissolution of forms. Probably because it was, in a way, a latecomer, it hasn't burnt out or been exhausted. It remains a fundamental source of truth about the contemporary world. It would be hard to say the same thing today of music or painting!

Cinema's chance is to be the latest addition, the seventh art. This has allowed it to plunder the others and stay young. I'm well aware that Godard maintains that cinema's been dead for a long time. I think this is a false thesis if taken literally. Of course, I see what he means. The power belonging to early cinema, and which marked it until the 1960s, can't easily be recuperated, essentially because of the technological saturation. There are too many parameters now, with the possibility of computer-generated images, of shooting whenever you want, of outdoor location shots. Such an inflation of parameters renders artistic mastery extremely difficult. Look at the images of Murnau's or Chaplin's films. I recently re-saw *City Lights* and was astounded by an aspect that I'd never before been struck by to such a degree, namely the film's extraordinary rigour, the control over the least element. Obviously, the fact of shooting in a studio, in black and white, means you're dealing with only a few parameters. You have all the time you need, you can concentrate on the parameters at hand. Cinema's progress is, as a result, what menaces it! Colour, large screen, and so on – fine, but how do you keep all that under control? It isn't an advantage to have a proliferation of means at your disposal. This is clearly shown by the great official painting of the nineteenth century, with its gigantic dimensions and technically perfect colours – the result of which is *art pompier*, a pompous, overblown, academic art. Well, we're in a period of overblown cinema.

– You've written, as regards the present and future of art, that 'art today must be as solidly unified as a demonstration, as surprising as a night raid and as elevated as a star.'[5]

– Yes, these are the three objectives, the three formulas of an affirmationist art – traces or promises of which can be found, moreover, in cinema. These three objectives are generally viewed as distinct in contemporary art. Coherence, for example, is considered to be incompatible with the element of surprise. Certainly, artists will work on surprising or astonishing the public, on disrupting habits, but the illogical, inconsistent, and even the evanescent nature of the thing will be taken as granted. Similarly, that which is surprising will be considered as incompatible with elevation or subjectivity. People will do anything to surprise with obscenity – pissing on stage or whatever you want. I'm not being critical here. I completely understand that these types of surprise – which lose their effect, in the long term – can be considered incompatible with coherence and elevation.

What's necessary, rather, is to try to align these three objectives. The long-standing ambition of art is threefold. First, to produce a coherence, including a new coherence, a coherence that's never existed before. This is the constructivist side of art. Second, to surprise, to be original. I'm not speaking of originality at any cost, but of the originality that can be integrated within the holistic construction that is the work of art. Third, elevation, which is to say the presence of the Idea, the proximity to the Idea: an elevation that is not contradictory with originality or coherence. This is why I say: 'unified like a demonstration, surprising like a night

[5] 'Manifesto of Affirmationism', trans. Barbara P. Fulks, *Lacanian Ink* 24/25, Spring 2005. (Translation modified.) Originally published as 'Troisième Esquisse d'un manifeste de l'affirmationnisme', *Circonstances* 2, Paris, Léo Scheer, 2004, pp. 81-105.

raid, elevated like a star.' But what interests me in these three metaphors is their connection.

– Is this connection what you yourself strove for as an artist, in *Calme bloc ici-bas*[6] for example, or in your theatre?

– This is certainly the case in *Calme bloc ici-bas*. I try there to wield a figure of prose that is subject to a system of coherent composition and rules, that possesses an effect of surprise, and that has something elevating about it insofar as it comprises an allegory of the contemporary world in which what is recounted is the crisis of the Idea. Indeed, the real, underlying subject of the book is the crisis of the Idea. As for theatre, I've tried, of course, to do something similar there.

The problem is that this is in no way an accepted view of the artwork. Either there are works that are coherent in a conventional sense and which forgo, as a result, the element of surprise, or there are elevated works that, relinquishing any attempt to surprise, end up in an academism. Or again, there are avant-garde works that use both surprise and deconstruction but at the price of a radical critique of both coherence and sublimity. When you try to maintain all three ambitions, you produce works that don't have an established space of construction and whose means of incorporation are weak. I'd point out in passing that, from my point of view, *Calme bloc* is the best thing I've done in my life. And it's undoubtedly also my sole deception. In my

[6] Alain Badiou, *Calme bloc ici-bas*, Paris, P.O.L., 1997. The title of Badiou's novel is drawn from Mallarmé's sonnet on Edgar Allan Poe. The sonnet's twelfth line, 'Calme bloc ici-bas chu d'un désastre obscur', was translated by Mallarmé himself as: 'Stern block here fallen from a mysterious disaster.' See Stephane Mallarmé, *Oeuvres completes*, ed. Bertrand Marchal, Paris, Gallimard [Pléiade], 1998, p. 1193. [Translator's note]

public life, I've known long periods of quasi-obscurity that haven't bothered me at all. Yet the fact that *Calme bloc* didn't attract any attention is perhaps the one thing that's hurt me a bit.

Philosophy and style, writing philosophy

– I'd like to ask a question about the state of mind you're in during the experience – or practice, or grace? – of writing. What's different about your state of mind when you write as a philosopher and when you write as an author?

– It's not at all the same thing. The difference between the two is radical. Writing philosophy is, to tell the truth, something I find relatively boring. My aim is, in fact, to give to things that are already formed in my thought a protocol of transmission that is already satisfactory to me, personally. As for the 'difficulty' my major texts are often attributed with, I believe that the passing of time will render justice to them on this point: they'll become classics like Kant's *Critique of Pure Reason* or Hegel's *Logic*. In the big books, in any case, I try to approximate as much as possible a detailed and argued expression of my thought; I'm in a rationality of transmission. In the other books, I seek, above all, to be clear and to ensure that the readers are fully on the level of what's being discussed; I may not always succeed in this but it's what I aim at!

When I write theatre, it's totally different. I don't know myself exactly what I'm going to write. The writing process is constitutive here of the thing itself. I'm no longer concerned with a protocol of transmission. I don't believe, on the other hand, that this applies to philosophy. What's involved in philosophy isn't created by its writing. The architecture of a philosophical idea exists in itself; it has its own autonomy. In this sense too, I'm a Platonist. Plato drew the conclusion from this, moreover, that the written word was secondary. In truth, the key point was the transmission of the Idea. Oral transmission was superior because it was accompanied by a transference effect that guaranteed or consolidated the transmission. My own approach to speaking is a bit along these lines. I see written texts as that which remains. In order to remain, you have to write! But in a novel or a play, that which exists is co-extensive to the writing. It hasn't any outside existence, whereas philosophical writing really transmits something outside of itself.

Moreover, you are acting in accordance with this idea yourself. Your project consists in elaborating a transmission of my philosophical discourse by means other than systematic writing and that borrow from orality since you start with a recording. On no account could this aspire to the level of an artwork. Whether you like it or not, philosophical writing – whatever might be its complexities, its effects of style or its literary affectations – is didactic writing. This remains the case even when it takes the form of a poem like Lucretius' *De Rerum Natura*. This trait of philosophy has to be accepted. For my part, I accept it without the slightest hesitation. Philosophy's tonality is one that aims at transmitting, convincing and changing intellectual subjectivities. The artwork functions totally differently.

– Is 'didactic' the right word for a book like *Theory of the Subject*?[7] Doesn't this possess a stylistic, Mallarmean, force that is patently obvious?

– *Theory of the Subject* attempted the slightly sophisticated exercise of transmuting oral expression into

---

[7] *Theory of the Subject*, trans. Bruno Bosteels, London, Continuum, 2009. Originally published as *Théorie du sujet*, Paris, Seuil, 1982.

written expression under conditions that were, in spite of everything, highly influenced by Lacan. This was the exercise of the seminar, in Lacan's sense, with ideas and constructions of a completely different nature than that of psychoanalysis. For this reason there is, indeed, an absolutely singular, stylistic aura in this book. I've the sentiment that *Theory of the Subject*, *Being and Event*[8] and *Logics of Worlds*[9] represent three different stylistic modalities. *Being and Event* is really very sober, consisting from start to finish of nothing other than systematic construction. *Logics of Worlds* is baroque, fragmented, taken up in deliberately particular examples. The fourth book, if I manage to write it, will be something else again. I envisage a lengthy, flowing prose, with a continuity unlike the systematic and architectonic continuity of *Being and Event*: a continuity that's in accordance with the perspective of the immanence of truths. Its title, moreover, will be *The Immanence of Truths*.

– A last question: What is the precise significance of style in philosophy? Why does a philosopher adopt such and such a style? You have just said yourself that you adopt specific styles for each of your major works.

– I think that through the style you attempt to resolve a problem. For you try to focus directly on a universal but this engages your own singularity at the same time. What's professed in this case is not a collective or anonymous universal. This is very different from scientific culture, where a collectivity decides the norm. You address yourself to your colleagues, who are the ones

---

[8] *Being and Event*, trans. Oliver Feltham, London, Continuum, 2005. Originally published as *L'Etre et l'événement*, Paris, Seuil, 1988.
[9] *Logics of Worlds*, trans. Alberto Toscano, London, Continuum, 2009. Originally published as *Logiques des mondes* (*L'Etre et l'événement*, tome 2), Paris, Seuil, 2006.

who are going to determine whether what you're saying is true or false. No style holds up in this case! You've got no chance of convincing them by your style that what you say is true! In philosophy, on the other hand, there's an ambiguity, which forms part of philosophy's impurity. We've mentioned the impurity of cinema. It so happens that I've upheld somewhere that there is a relation between philosophy and cinema – which is, precisely, impurity. Cinema proposes attempted, or real, works of art, made up of extraordinarily heterogeneous elements. Philosophy, for its part, also uses almost anything: citations of poems, mathematical demonstrations, or myths as in the style of Plato. It does the same thing cinema does. Philosophy is the cinema of thought!

To reply now more directly to your question: style is what attempts to hold together what is, in principle, philosophy's absolutely universal vocation and the fact that there are few undertakings that are as radically singular. For we only know the system of so-and-so or such-and-such and not any universal philosophy. Here, then, is a history of universality formed entirely of a collection of singularities. This finds expression in the writing. Even if you place yourself in the strictest form of universality, in formal protocols like Descartes' *Principles*, Spinoza's *Ethics*, or even certain passages of *Being and Event* that are of a strict demonstrative modality, you never lose sight of the fact that this is signed. Philosophy is, on the one hand, the cinema of thought and, on the other, the signed universal. So, there are two definitions I'm offering you! Style is, of course, the signature. 'It's by Alain Badiou.' Ideally of course, it should be professed in an anonymous fashion but, concretely, it attests that it's by Alain Badiou.

4

Sciences

– Technology and its relation to science could serve as our starting point. First, do you share Heidegger's bleak view of technological progress, conceived as 'the forgetting of being', a darkening of the human condition? This darkening seems all the more ineluctable given that Heidegger makes technological development a 'historical'[1] fact – an irreducible component, in other words, of human destiny as such.

[1] The French term employed here by Tarby – *historial* – constitutes the standard rendering in French of the German *geschichtlich* as this is used by Heidegger in contradistinction to *historisch*. While *historisch* refers to the objective configuration of chronological 'facts' and relations, and is thus correlated to what Heidegger calls a 'science of History' (*Historie*), *geschichtlich* is a word closely related to *geschicklich* (from the substantive *Geschick*, notably found in Heidegger's expression *Seingeschick*: the *sending* or *destiny* of being) and bears both the sense of 'history' and 'occurrence'. *Geschichtlich* designates, as a result, the epochality of being as this is disclosed in 'human' destiny. Most English translations of Heidegger's works render *geschichtlich* as 'historical' and *historisch* as either 'historic' or 'historiological'. The translation of 'historial' here as 'historical' thus follows this convention. [Translator's note]

– I don't think you can impute technological progress as such to an ontological, historical figure. After all, it's technological progress that makes it possible for humankind to expand as a species. As for the darkening in cause, this is not a question of technology per se – that is, the totality of science's practical outcomes – but of its being aligned on merchandise. Science can't itself be reduced to technology; it has an autonomy of truth. Yet, there exists an entire network of science's practical uses, which, while not prescribed by science, are nonetheless made possible by it. It's not technology that one should rail against, therefore, but science's being subjected to the system of its possible practical outcomes – its subjection to the capitalist mode of production.

The theme of scientific truth is itself, in fact, obscured, as a result. In this sense, there is a 'darkening' by technology, which is not due to technology but to the fact that science is obscured as a truth procedure. What brings this about is the way scientific ideas and their practical outcomes are violently and obligatorily aligned on, or reoriented towards, mercantile consumption. This entails the production, at worst, of an incredible number of things that are ugly, useless, and appalling, and, at best, of things that are useful but produced in a totally anarchic manner. The norm is, indeed, neither the useful nor the beautiful, but the sellable.

– What do think, then, of the relation Heidegger establishes between technological progress and 'the forgetting of being'?

– As far as the question of 'the forgetting of being' is concerned, I obviously don't share Heidegger's disposition towards this. There is, in Heidegger, the idea of a lost origin that I believe has to be dispensed with. There is nothing in technological development that pertains to the lost origin. What could, moreover, this lost origin possibly be? The auroral Greek world, a world of slavery, of ferocious wars and indiscriminate massacres? It's a typically German invention! I don't adhere to any of this in the slightest. Nevertheless, Heidegger was a great thinker, despite his also being a Nazi petit-bourgeois. He had the insight that the technological appropriation of science could only find a relay or an alternative through something that was of the order of thought – he wouldn't have said 'the Idea' since he loathed this word that led back to Platonism. Heidegger understood that the crisis was that of thought. Unfortunately, he didn't see that thought is nothing if it is not governed or commanded by the possibility of a politics of emancipation for the whole of humanity. He didn't see this because he was an old reactionary! This doesn't diminish the interest of many of his analyses: for example, on temporality, the phenomenology of anguish, contemporaneity (even if on this point he misses no doubt that which is essential), figures of alienation, the history of philosophy, poetry, and so on.

What ultimately sets me against Heidegger is that he accepts taking a position in the struggle between tradition and merchandise. In this struggle, he is, in his sophisticated and complicated fashion, on the side of tradition. Yet, it's necessary to be on neither one side nor the other – this is what's hard. The whole problem is to refuse the choice that's imposed upon us: tradition or modernity, tradition or merchandise. A situation has to be created that escapes this alternative. Even if the things in the world well and truly obey this alternative, you mustn't let yourself be structured by this opposition. The crisis of emancipatory politics, the crisis of the Idea, consists precisely in being entrapped in this opposition and in thinking that there isn't any choice other than either an apologia of the contemporary democratic world or the tensions over identity proper to tradition.

– For your part, you refer essentially to mathematics and logic rather than to physics or biology. The question of the place physics and biology have in your work is a strongly debated one. Some feel that there is a lacuna in this respect.

– The objection according to which physics and biology aren't present in my philosophy isn't sufficiently fleshed out. First of all, I absolutely recognize physics as a truth procedure. As far as biology is concerned, I'm less sure since the scientific component of biology belongs to the field of chemistry, while the rest of biological research is, like medicine, an empiricism gone wild. There are very few theoretical propositions in biology. To my mind, it hasn't made any significant progress since Darwin. Darwin elaborated what I call *a body of thought* [*une pensée*], where it's really a matter of neither philosophy nor science but of a powerful rational framework that created the possible horizon of a science without, strictly speaking, entering into this. This is very characteristic of the nineteenth century, which saw three great bodies of thought: Marx for history, Darwin for natural history and Freud for the unconscious. These thinkers' capacity of revitalizing and turning things upside down, their predictive prowess, as well as their overthrowing of taboos, are all things I greatly admire. Yet, who today would dare to uphold that a science of history really exists? There is a framework of thought that makes it possible to eliminate false discourses. Darwinism makes it possible to eliminate creationism, but it hasn't as yet constituted a theorized science of the evolution of biological forms. Apart from Darwinism, which is a matter of the history of biological forms, biology is chemistry – and a chemistry that is still very much in the dark. There's the observation of experimentally highly localized causes and effects. What life is hasn't been able to be set out – it remains an extremely elusive concept.

There's not, however, the slightest shadow of a doubt that physics is a science. I think, moreover, that mathematization is an absolute criterion of scientificity. The smaller the mathematical component, the larger the hermeneutic element becomes. Physics has, what's more, become mathematized to a spectacular degree. In quantum physics, mathematics is no longer a language, it's the thing itself. Without the equations, you understand nothing at all. All the attempts to fuel quantum physics by any sort of intuition have, additionally, led to rather pitiful mental constructions or to neo-religious positions that are patently obscurantist.

– Yes, one can think of all those telepathic visions that use quantum physics as a justification. That said, mystical views of set theory can also be found.

– Admittedly, mathematized mysticism has existed since the beginning of mathematics. Pythagoreanism was, it would seem, a mysticism of numbers. Nevertheless, to come back to your question on physics, I'd be fully able to understand that people object to the absence of physics in my philosophy were this objection philosophically localized. You can't just point out that there isn't any physics. There of lots of other things that aren't there either! I'm far from having elaborated a general aesthetics. It would also be possible to object that I don't deal much with architecture – even if I speak a bit about Brasilia – or with contemporary painting, installations, and so on. Physics isn't there – fine. But what's the philosophical protocol of the question? What conceptual zone do I put forward or construct that would be essentially modified or opened up to truly new questions by physics being brought to bear on it?

It's absolutely fundamental to point out that physics, contrary to mathematics, theorizes particular worlds. Physics speaks of worlds that we know, including by the means of our sense organs, and in which we find our protocols of empirical verification. Moreover, physics functions in compatibility with general ontology. This is the reason it's mathematized furthermore, because mathematics is ontology. As a result, it's normal that the determination of particular phenomena in a particular world encompasses being qua being and its mathematizable multiplicities. That said, I've never encountered an interlocutor who has said to me: 'on such and such a philosophical point proposed by you, on being as much as on appearing, the developments of classical or contemporary physics introduce a radical differentiation.'

I'd note finally that the philosophical uses of physics have, throughout history, been not of a productive nature but of a limitative one. They have always introduced a restrictive and critical conception of knowledge. It was Kant who launched this tendency. From Kant up to Popper, the determination of the conditions of knowledge by physics was so strict and rigid that it has ended up making room for religion or all sorts of complementary idealism. Kant pretty much said: 'in all matters relating to moral and religious truths, I've had to substitute faith for knowledge.' This is not philosophical progress! The reason for this is that, if you start from physics, that of Newton in Kant's case, that of Einstein in Popper's, you start from transcendental laws of a particular world and you take the particularities of this world for the limits of knowledge in general.

– I'm going to try to put an objection to you using an example. A vase that falls to the ground can break in many different ways, mathematically. There's a whole set of possibilities. But, concretely, physically, it will break at that particular moment in one way and not another. Here then is effectivity, the real . . . Isn't everything that is mathematic, physical? Isn't this what has to be thought?

– I fully understand. Yet what does 'effectivity' mean in the context of the general theory I'm proposing? 'Effective' can mean nothing other than being pertinent in respect of a given mundane transcendental. I uphold that physics is a regional theory of appearing. Nothing says that it is a general theory! Since it's necessary for it to have physical correlates, it is situated in the transcendental of a given world and, as a result, in a particular mathematical-logical whole [*ensemble*] which lets itself be tested by experience. Certainly, it's a science! I don't deny this. Yet, it's a science with an inevitably limited philosophical impact because its mundane scale is always determined in advance. From this point of view, it is true that philosophy is not, for its part, a theory of effectivity. It's always a science that is a theory of effectivity.

You are correct, then: physics raises the question of effectivity. Yet for me, this question is settled by the fact that an effectivity is always a localization, and a localization, when all is said and done, is a transcendental. Basically, what is physics? It's the development in the real, if it's possible to put it this way, of the transcendental of the material world we're in. Physics oscillates, in this way, between a hyper-local determination – that of the absolutely singular phenomena of microphysics – and a determination on a far vaster scale, which is astrophysics. Microphysics can for the instant only be made sense of mathematically, while astrophysics, despite its very significant mathematical component, is roughly equivalent to Darwin's theory of evolution. It's a body of thought in which assumptions and hermeneutics have a large place. It's not known, for example, what two-thirds of the matter in our universe is exactly. For there to be the least step forward at the present time, it's necessary to have recourse to gigantic machines. All of which, in terms of these enormous empirical requirements, shows that, while its mathematization indicates physics to have a certain degree of universality

– a universality demonstrating that it 'touches' ontology – physics cannot claim to have a philosophical role comparable to that of mathematics, and by far!

– I've precisely a question concerning these gigantic machines, like the Large Hadron Collider at the CERN,[2] near Geneva, where thousands of physicists are looking for the Higgs boson, the graviton and other fundamental particles. These machines have been spoken of as 'philosophical instruments'. Can physics be said to be returning to the problems of Greek ontology? Isn't physics becoming an ontology?

– To my mind, the questions involved here aren't ontological but regional ones: those dealing with the exact nature of the transcendental of the material world we know. They're not about being qua being, but about the determinate being of phenomena on a strictly material scale, and they're able to be tested empirically. It is very striking to see that these questions make headway now not so much with new hypotheses but with new machines. Physics has, moreover, been in permanent crisis since the 1930s. The physicists who are truly loyal recognize this. No one knows exactly what quantum physics is. Its mathematical framework is reliable, but, as a physical framework, it remains altogether odd.

Physics is split in two. There's no unification of forces within a coherent body of thought and, as a result, there's a headlong rush on two flanks: the development,

[2] CERN – the name given to the world's largest particle physics laboratory – originally stood for *Conseil Européen pour la Recherche Nucléaire* (European Council for Nuclear Research), which was a provisional council for setting up the laboratory, established by twelve European governments in 1952. Although this council was dissolved in 1954, when the organization operating the laboratory became the European Organization for Nuclear Research, the acronym CERN has been retained. [Translator's note]

on one side, of mathematical models that are so intricate that their empirical validity is without any protocol of verification and, on the other, experimental techniques that are so cumbersome that their results pose more problems than they resolve. This obvious crisis situation doesn't make me deviate an inch as regards my position that physics is a science, but confirms that this is a gigantically big science dealing with the contingency of a given world. This is why it's not a matter of ontology. Indeed, so much is it a question of the contingent that it's completely possible to envisage returning to the ancient idea of there existing other worlds, organized according to completely different laws.

– Physics is, then, related to our animal constitution, whereas mathematics pertains solely to the order of pure thought?

– As regards thought, it so happens that I'm a partisan of emergence theory. Life is a universe that cannot be reduced to matter, while thought is a universe irreducible to life. Thought is, in any case, an activity *sui generis*. Yet when you're at the border of thought and the empirical limits that are proper to us, as is the case with physics, you are in a figure of thought that refers to something other than itself. This other thing must well and truly be understood as relative to the transcendental of the world in which the animals that we are live. From this perspective, physics remains linked to our animal singularity. This is not so for mathematics. I maintain that any thinking being whatsoever, regardless of its organic make-up, regardless of its material site, would understand mathematics. Just as the theorem asserting the existence of an infinity of prime numbers, demonstrated 2,500 years ago, conserves both its truth and its beauty for us, so any thinking being would understand both this truth and this beauty in the same way we do. Such a being might perhaps be stronger than we are in mathematics, or perhaps not; it might have other ideas or have discovered sectors of mathematics that we can't even imagine. But we could discuss with it on perfectly equal terms of thought. This was what Spinoza thought, as did, in another register, Leibniz: mathematics is sufficiently absolute for us to be able to discuss it with God.

– A topic of conversation in common – that's already something!

– I'd say that, as regards the topics of conversation between God and human beings, there are two camps. There are those who think that, with him, we could only discuss mathematics, and those who think that we could only discuss morality. It's hard to think, however, that we could discuss, for example, music with God. What the ears of God could be is not very clear. We could perhaps discuss physics, but we would, then, hear God say: 'Well, yes, that's how it is solely because I created that world that way!' Morality, on the other hand, is something we envisage as possible to discuss with God.

– I heard an academic one day describe you as a Leibniz without God.

– This is possibly one way of putting it. Though, if you remove God from Leibniz's system, you have a series of repercussions that are devastating. The world is no longer the best of worlds but absolutely contingent, and if it is absolutely contingent then the principle of pre-established harmony has to be taken away, and if pre-established harmony is taken away then human action is no longer governed . . . One thing leading to another, everything starts to come apart at the seams. What's clear in any case with Leibniz is that he was, indeed, convinced that we could speak about mathematics with God. He even deduced from this that the world was the result of a mathematical calculation. He tried to mathematize physics at an ontological level. He has a mathematized ontology of the world. In his case, physics effectively becomes ontology.

– There's no God in your work, of course. Some people find it hard at times to understand how an atheism can be constructed on mathematics. We mentioned earlier that mathematics can give rise to mysticism. Others would see order and beauty in it. What is the relation in your work, then, between the void and atheism, on the one hand, and multiplicities and mathematics, on the other?

– As far as mathematics is concerned, my remarks on the subject are to be taken in the strictest sense. Mathematics is the thought of the multiple as such. It's from this that the principles of order discovered by mathematics are exclusively deduced. There is not any more order in mathematics than there is in the concept of pure multiplicity as set out on the basis of this sole idea: something belongs to something. The consequences of this are enumerated and appropriate axiomatic decisions are based on what these consequences outline. I took great care in *Being and Event* to comment on each of these axioms one after the other. I discuss all of the axioms of set theory and show to what philosophical space, what space of thought, they pertain. As a result, mathematics is simply the fact that the complexity of pure being is a complexity that lets itself be rationally mastered. This order is quite simply that of the complexity offered by pure being in the form of incomposed multiplicity or, in other words, of multiplicity that doesn't refer to fundamental atomic units.

– Finally, have you found yourself confronted at times by objections or critiques concerning your thought of mathematics that have seemed strong to you?

– What can be objected to, though this rarely happens, is my choice of the strongest kind of set theory. The type of set theory I put forward goes as far as it's able to without encountering any formal contradictions that would annihilate its conceptual framework. A hypothesis on being is involved here – namely, the hypothesis that in our thinking of the multiple, there is no need for us, on our part, to introduce external limitations on this thought. This obviously implies, for example, that we accept the existence 'in act' of infinite multiplicities. It's well known that the intuitionists don't agree with this and that classical mathematics was very reticent in this respect. Are there very large cardinal numbers, huge multiplicities? I say yes, on principle. I consider that being, in its multiform possibility, hasn't to be limited by diktats that merely reflect the difficulty of our empirical intuition to follow the creative force of concepts.

Those who state that they don't take any account of the infinite because they have to remain 'bound to an operative procedure' and other things of this type, or those who refuse to admit cardinals higher than natural numbers, are people who are, in fact, doing physics: they're measuring being according to the limits of their imagination. I think that the power of mathematics lies in it's never letting itself be limited by the finitude of our intuition. If there aren't any contradictions, if it continues to work, then full steam ahead! This is, of course, a point of view totally opposed to philosophy's critical tradition – its Kantian, neo-Kantian, intuitionist, tradition and so on. This tradition always consists in saying: 'Careful, we can't go any further than the intuition that accompanies our experience.' The fact is that, while you can well have a perfectly rational definition of a measurable or ineffable cardinal, you can always go whistle for an intuition of it!

The philosopher can and must love this mathematical world where the concept is so pure and so strong that it renders intuition ridiculous. It was already the case in ancient Greece that the discovery of irrational numbers rendered ridiculous the banal intuition of what a number was. This kind of sovereignty of the concept is like the mathematical, and hence ontological, image of what Plato calls an Idea.

5

Philosophy

**The Immanence of Truths: the third volume after
Being and Event and Logics of Worlds**

– Let's now address the question of knowledge and,
hence, philosophy. I'd like to frame this in terms of joy
– the joy of knowing – which is the *affect*, moreover,
that you associate with the condition of science. We
might think here of the contemplative life in Aristotle
or Spinoza's beatitude. I'd remark in passing that you
don't use the term 'joy' in your analysis of the amorous
condition.

– The figure of love, as we've mentioned, is one of the
truth procedures. This joint protocol of knowledge, this
vision of the world from the point of view of the two,
that love is, does, I believe, have a form of positive affect
specific to it. I've chosen, as regards the affects linked
to the truth procedures overall, to speak of enthusiasm
for politics, joy for scientific knowledge, pleasure for art
and happiness for love. It's true that I've not described
these affects by going into a phenomenology of them. I
will probably remedy this if I manage to write the third

volume of the series, the comprehensive title of which is *Being and Event: The Immanence of Truths*. This book is going to bear on everything that occurs for a given individual when she or he is incorporated within a procedure of truth, when she or he is seized by the Idea. I'll have to address new points, particularly that of the difference between these affects: happiness is not pleasure, pleasure is not joy.

– I'd like to know a bit more about this work that you're envisaging: *The Immanence of Truths*.

– Let's first put things into perspective. We can do this fairly easily. *Being and Event*, which can be considered the first part of a three-stage construction, is principally concerned with the question of being. What is the position regarding being, being qua being as Aristotle said? What about the ways and means of knowing it? My ontological proposition is that being qua being is a pure multiplicity, i.e., a multiplicity that is not composed of atoms. Being is obviously composed of elements but these elements are multiplicities that are themselves composed of multiplicities. There is, that said, an endpoint, which is not at all the One – the One would necessarily be an atom – but the void. So, that's what I propose regarding being. As for the knowledge of being, I propose that ontology – the discourse on being – be identified with mathematics. *Being and Event* develops, moreover, a theory of truths in counterpoint. This is a formal theory of truths: truths are, like all things, multiplicities; it's a matter of knowing what kind. The book deals, therefore, both with a theory of being and a theory of truths; all this, in a theory of the pure multiple.

The second part of this construction, *Logics of Worlds*, tackles the question of appearing – 'being' and 'appearing' are, moreover, completely classical problems in the history of philosophy. It consists in a theory of that which, of being, appears in given worlds and forms relations between objects of these worlds. I propose calling this part of the whole construction, a 'logic'. It's a logic insofar as it doesn't bear on the composition of that which is, but on the relations that are established between all the things that appear locally in worlds. Consequently, after a theory of being, this is a theory of being-there – to employ a terminology close to that of Hegel – which is to say, of being as this is placed and arrayed in a particular world.

In *Logics of Worlds*, the question of truth is obviously taken up again. *Being and Event* dealt with the being of truths qua generic multiplicities. With *Logics of Worlds*, we broach the question of real bodies and the logic of their relations, focusing, in particular, on the appearing of truths. If everything that appears in a world is a body, the question of the body of a truth has to be addressed. This second volume is, then, to a large extent intended as a theory of bodies, which is a theory of the body of truths, whereas the first volume was intended as a theory of truths qua generic multiplicities.

The third volume intends to examine things from the point of view of truths. The first volume asks: what about truths in relation to being? The second: what about truths in relation to appearing? The third will ask: what about being and appearing from the point of view of truths? In this way, I will have examined the question from all sides.

A truth, from the human or anthropological point of view, is composed of individual incorporations within much larger ensembles. I'd like to know how the world and individuals of this world are presented and arrayed when they are examined from within the very process of truths. This is a question that reverses, as it were, the perspective of the first two volumes. We asked what truths were from the standpoint of being and from the point of view of the world; now we're asking what the position is regarding being and the world from the point of view of truths.

There are, of course, indications along these lines in the first two works. *Being and Event*, in particular, contains a fairly complicated theory of truths returning to the world in the figure of knowledge. I propose there to call knowledge, new knowledge or the creation of knowledge, the way in which a truth throws new light on the ontological situation. It's like in Plato: we accede to the Idea by leaving the cave, but it's necessary to go back down into the cave in order to illuminate it by the Idea.

– At the cost of taking a certain number of risks!

– Yes, it's when you go back into the cave and take a position on the world as it is and its prevailing ideologies from the perspective of what you consider to be truths that you run the greatest risk. I've already dealt with this question of returning in *Being and Event* under the name of the theory of forcing: you force a transformation of knowledge on the basis of truth. This is a relatively complex theory, as is already the case, in fact, with Plato's theory of going back into the cave. Ultimately Plato doesn't say all that much except that the return is very risky and very difficult: there's no knowing what will happen.

– It's necessary to be forced to return; otherwise you'd stay in the calm domain of the contemplation of truths.

– Yes, and that's why the term of forcing is completely appropriate. It's not a natural or spontaneous procedure. *Logics of Worlds*, for its part, doesn't contain a theory of forcing but sets out a theory of the closely knit relations between the singularity of the world and the universality of a truth through an investigation into the empirical and concrete conditions, within the domain of appearing, that govern the construction of truth-bodies.

I maintain that truth is a body. As such, it is made up of what there is, which is to say other individual bodies, and this is what is called an incorporation. This incorporation sheds light on the way in which a truth proceeds in a world and on its relation with the materials of this world itself, namely bodies and language. As you're aware, I start off in *Logics of Worlds* from the formula: 'In a world, there are only bodies and languages, except that there are truths.' I then go on to a first examination of this 'except that': truths are also bodies and language, subjectivizable bodies. In order to throw light on truths' relation to bodies and languages, I use a notion that is the equivalent of forcing in *Being and Event*, namely the concept of compatibility. A truth-body is composed, in fact, of elements that are compatible in both a technical and elementary sense: they let themselves be dominated by a common element.

Basically, a truth is always a unified multiplicity, governed or organized by something that makes compatible that which may not have necessarily been so at the start. To take a very simple example: the elaboration of what a political party was consisted largely in creating a theory in which workers and intellectuals were compatible, and in which class differences that aren't normally compatible would be rendered compatible through politics. Theories like Gramsci's theory of organic intellectuals are of this type. They don't simply deal with class differences as conflict but also create compatibilities between classes where these didn't previously exist – as with a theory of class alliances, for example. You find the same type of situation in aesthetics. A work of art – considered as a subject – creates compatibilities between things that had been considered non-compatible or completely separate. A painting creates compatibilities between colours that seemingly weren't meant to go together or between forms that were disparate. It integrates forms and colours in compatibilities of a higher order.

In short, the concept of forcing, on the ontological
level, and the concept of compatibility, on the phenomenological level, already deal with the relation between
truth and the situation in which truth is operative. The
third volume, should I really have the courage to write
it, will systematize all that. It will set itself up, as it were,
in the different types of truth in order to ask: What
happens when a whole world is approached from the
point of view of truth? What happens ontologically
when the point of view adopted is that of generic multiplicities on the ordinary, indifferent multiplicities that
ontologically make up a situation?

To come back to your question at the start about joy,
I can tell you that I'm going to deal with the specific
affects that indicate, on the individual level, the process
of incorporation. What is amorous happiness? What is
aesthetic pleasure? What is political enthusiasm? What
is scientific joy, or beatitude? Joy will, like the other
three affects, be systematically studied in *The Immanence of Truths*.

– How will this book be structured?

– I plan on broadly elaborating first of all, in more
precise, technical terms, the problem that I've just sche-
matically set out. I then envisage a second part that will
identify the general protocols indicating relations to the
world from the point of view of truths. This will yield,
therefore, a general theory of individual incorporation
and the affects that indicate this. Here, I'll be looking
at questions like: What is the opening of the world from
the point of view of truths? What is an obstacle? A
victory? A failure? A creation? A third part will re-
examine things, truth procedure by truth procedure, in
proposing a systematic theory of art, science, love and
politics. Such a theory isn't found anywhere in my work
even if there have been intimations of it in numerous

places. This, then, is the plan – ideal, in its present absence – of *The Immanence of Truths*.

– Are you proposing, then, to unify the four conditions of philosophy? What form would this unity take?

– I intend to propose a theory of what these procedures have in common and of the unity they're capable of virtually. This will precisely be the object of the second part. It will consist in taking up a theory of truths but this time from the point of view of truths themselves. It will involve asking what identifies them in themselves and no longer what distinguishes them from anonymous being or from objects in the world. But it will also involve continuing my interrogation of philosophy. As you know, in the *Manifesto for Philosophy*,[1] I define it as that which creates a site of 'compossibility', or co-existence, for the four conditions. It remains to be examined if philosophy doesn't additionally depend on a figure of life that would integrate these procedures. This is a question I'm asked quite often, and I mean to tackle it head-on.

It amounts in a way to asking: what is a full life? I'm not speaking solely of a true life, which is a question I address, for that matter, at the end of *Logics of Worlds*. The true life – declared absent by Rimbaud but which I maintain can be present – consists in living under the sign of the Idea, which is to say living under the sign of effective incorporation. The other question is related but distinct: Is there an Idea of ideas, that is, an Idea of

[1] *Manifesto for Philosophy*, trans. Norman Madarasz, Albany, SUNY Press. Originally published as: *Manifeste pour la philosophie*, Paris, Seuil, 1989. See also *Second Manifesto for Philosophy*, trans. Louise Burchill, London and New York, Polity, 2011. Originally published as: *Second manifeste pour la philosophie*, Paris, Fayard, 2009.

the full life? We return in this way to the aim of ancient wisdom, taking up in our turn this quintessentially initial aspiration to a life that is not only marked by the Idea and by truth but by the idea of a fulfilled life, a life in which everything that could be experimented with, as far as truth is concerned, has been.

– Can we speak then of a philosophical *subject* or a *subject* of philosophy? Would this be the, perhaps absent, centre of the four conditions?

– The centre of these four conditions is philosophy itself, and not a philosophical subject, the existence of which is uncertain. The question you've raised will, however, also haunt this third volume. I have always fought against the thesis that philosophy was a truth procedure like the others. It can't be like the others because it depends on their existence, whereas neither art nor science, nor love, nor politics, depends on the existence of philosophy. As a result, it's obvious that philosophy is apart from the four types of truth procedures. That said, it remains an open question whether the place of a philosophical subject can be pointed to. If there is a philosophical subject, what does this consist in? What does having access to philosophy consist in? What does being in philosophy consist in? Certainly, there isn't any philosophical incorporation in the sense of the incorporation that's found in the case of political activists or artists, scientists and lovers. And yet philosophy does give access to a coherent thought, and not nothing. The question remains open: if a subject of philosophy is presumed to exist, what place would it have? Is it, as you suggest, an absent centre? It's clear that philosophy proposes a general doctrine of what a subject of truth is. But in what way do you enter into this philosophical proposition and how do you sustain yourself there? In what way does it enable a new perspective on truth procedures? And, finally, how can it open the path to the true life or the full life? These are the questions I'm going to raise. It's clear that my way of approaching these questions has always been somewhat hesitant. I'm faced with an unresolved problem. It's not because my philosophy is systematic that it pretends to have resolved all the problems!

– You're dissatisfied, then, with some points of your philosophy?

– Up to now, in any case, I've tended to approach some problems negatively, by rejecting rather than proposing. Thus, I've rejected the sophistic thesis according to which philosophy is a general unification of things only because it's a general rhetoric. The linguistic turn of the twentieth century essentially led to a type of doctrine that assimilates philosophy to a general rhetoric. This can go as far as the position adopted by Barbara Cassin, according to which there isn't ontology but only logology, such that it would be language that carves out or constitutes everything that has been envisaged as being. The twentieth century showed a trend that increasingly focused on the creative power of language, and which was academic, critical and anti-dogmatic all at the same time. Derrida was fully part of this. In my view, this trend turns philosophy into a general rhetoric – as subtle and as modern a rhetoric as you could want. Yet, as I've stated several times, that's not the register in which I place myself. I position myself in the discussion between Plato and the sophists. As established by the *Cratylus*, we philosophers begin with things and not with words.

Negatively, then, I've already taken a series of positions on the access to philosophy. More affirmatively, I've designated what I've called philosophical operations – with my speaking, as such, not of events but of operations. It seemed to me that two of these were impossible to contest. First, the operations of

identification: philosophy detects truths, in particular
the truths of its time, by constructing a new concept of
what a truth is. The second operation consists in philosophy's rendering truth's diverse and heterogeneous
modalities compossible through the category of truth.
We're dealing here with a function of discernment and
a function of unification. Philosophy has always been
wedged between the two. Discernment results in a critical conception, distinguishing between what is true and
what is not true, whereas unification results in different
uses of the category of totality and system.

I uphold these two classical functions of philosophy.
I've always maintained that I'm a classical philosopher.
I show that philosophy elaborates, contemporaneously
with its conditions, categories of truth by means of
which it is able to discern and isolate these conditions,
and show that they are irreducible to the way of functioning of the ordinary world. Moreover, it tries in a
way to think a concept of the contemporary, by
showing how the conditions comprise an epoch, a
dynamic of thought, in which each and every subject is
inscribed.

All this, I've already done. Yet, it's necessary to go
further and ask what philosophy's relation to life is.
This question is fundamental. If you can't say what
purpose philosophy serves from the point of view of the
true life, then it's just one more academic discipline. The
third volume will attempt, then, to make it possible to
tackle this question head-on. This will involve taking up
Plato's question of the relation between philosophy and
happiness.

– In your proximity to Plato, isn't there something like
a very profound intuition, which you would share with
this philosopher, regarding the subject and truth? An
intuition that would be hard to communicate – I'm
thinking in particular of Book VI of the *Republic*, where
Plato seems to declare that the nature of the Good is

impossible to put into words – and which would prompt you now to write *The Immanence of Truths*?

– I think your question is completely relevant. I myself am struck by the fact that my way of dealing, up to now, with truths and, therefore, the subject – which, as the protocol of a truth's orientation, is absolutely linked to truth – has been purely differential. I've asked what type of multiplicity a truth is. What is it that differentiates it from ordinary multiplicities? This is what *Being and Event* fundamentally deals with. I was already at that time concerned with exception. If a truth is an exception to the laws of the world, it must be possible to explain what this exception consists in. If you are in the domain of ontology, of the theory of being, of the mathematical theory of being, you must be able to explain mathematically what type of multiplicity is specific to truths. In referring to set theory and the theorems of Cohen, I show that this multiplicity is generic. In other words, it's a multiplicity that can't be thought by means of the forms of knowledge available to us. There isn't any predicate in available forms of knowledge that can be used to identify it. This is what Cohen's technique allows us to show: that there exists an indiscernible multiplicity, which cannot be discerned by the predicates that circulate in forms of knowledge. In this way, truth eludes knowledge at the level of its very being. This seems to be a positive determination of truths: they are generic multiplicities. But on close examination, it turns out to be a negative determination: they are multiplicities that cannot be reduced to available knowledge. Truth is defined, then, by way of a differential factor and not a factor that is intrinsic to truth.

In *Logics of Worlds*, truth is defined as a subjectivizable body. As such, it has a number of specific characteristics, but the main one is that the protocol of this body's construction entails that everything comprising it is compatible. This compability is, however, basically only a relational characteristic of what a truth is. Within a truth, there is a relation of compatibility between all its elements. This is an objective characteristic. In both cases, I've arrived, then, at a precise objective determination of, respectively, a truth's being and its appearing. But what's missing is, precisely, a subjective determination. All this doesn't tell us what a truth is as lived within the procedure of truth, that is, what it is for the subject of truth itself.

My answers to these questions remain, in my view, too functional. I state that the subject is, on the ontological level, a point or a local moment of truth. On the phenomenological level, I state that a subject is a function of orientation in respect of the construction of a subjectivizable body. These are functional definitions that remain, themselves, objective. It's now necessary to arrive at something that materializes, inscribes and organizes the protocol of truth, as viewed immanently this time, which is to say subjectivized as such. In *Theory of the Subject*, I distinguished between 'subjective process' and 'subjectivization'. Taking up the terms of this distinction, I would say that *Being and Event* and *Logics of Worlds* contain decisive things on the 'subjective process', but 'subjectivization' remains obscure and dealt with in a negative and purely differential fashion. Subjectivization is the way in which one subjectivizes the protocol of truth internally. What's lacking is an intuition of what a subjectivization is.

– Will there be a new formalism in *The Immanence of Truths* or a combination of formalisms that you have already used?

– For the moment, I know one thing in any case – that it's going to entail a formal transformation of the category of negation. If a truth's subjective protocols are made up of the incorporations or the rallying by individuals, what then has to be asked is how does individual difference function within the protocol of truth. This is a question that has always interested me. Let's take a very simple example. Two people are looking at a painting. There will be a fragment of incorporation; a fragment that is indicated by a certain affect, an intellectual effort, and the immobilization of the gaze upon the painting. I'm putting myself in the position of the spectator rather than the creator in order to indicate that a truth is constantly open to incorporation. Is this act of subjectivization in which incorporation consists, the same for the two spectators? Is it a matter of identity or of compatibility? We can't say in any case that the duality internal to this experience – and millions of people can, moreover, participate in this same experience – is going to disrupt the unity of the subject. How is this possible? Much of the scepticism concerning truths has its roots in this type of experience. Everyone has his own truth, according to Pirandello! 'Everyone has his own truth' implies that there isn't any truth at all. In the case of a painting, a unique object will be broken up according to the perceptions of the various parties.

That said, why does this lead to the problem of negation? The reason is that the whole problem is what type of negation this difference refers to. Everyone sees the painting in his or her own way; one person's perception isn't the same as another's. But what does this 'isn't' mean? What breaks up perception and leads to scepticism is the idea that this 'isn't' is a classical negation, i.e., that one of the perceptions can, and must, be contradictory with the other.

– What theory of negation do you plan on referring to in order to avoid this sceptical consequence of ordinary negation?

– The theory of paraconsistent negation, the third type of logic (after classical and intuitionistic logic) discovered by the Brazilian Da Costa, in which the principle of contradiction doesn't hold. The new formalism that will, then, be introduced on a large scale in this third volume will be paraconsistent negation, which explicitly contradicts the principle of non-contradiction. This makes it possible, in the case of a truth, for contradictory perceptions to co-exist without disrupting this truth's unity. This interests me all the more since a problem of this type is found at the core of love if you accept, which is my position, that in order to fully understand love you have to start from the co-existence of a feminine position and a masculine position – two positions that are, in some respects, completely separate.

– The problem of negation would come up again in this way, then. Mightn't it also come up again in the four conditions?

– Yes, you're quite right. As a result, whereas the main formalism consisted, in *Being and Event*, of set theory and Cohen's theorem, and, in *Logics of Worlds*, of the theory of sheaves or the topologization of logic, the main formalism in the third volume will be paraconsistent logic, with a whole meditation on the limits of the principle of non-contradiction.

Philosophy and transmission

– I'd like to ask you now a more general question, which will no doubt take us back to Plato. Couldn't it be said that all philosophers start from a subjective contact with truth – their personal point of encounter with truth, as it were? This point is what they would try to transmit through their philosophy. Yet at the same time, they know, deep down inside, that this point can't be transmitted since it's their uniquely own contact with truth.

Wouldn't this explain, in particular, why Plato finds it so difficult to define the Idea of the Good? Doesn't one run the risk of arriving, at this point, at the ineffable?

– Yes, a point of ineffability is, indeed, reached there. This happens in a lot of philosophical configurations. A point is reached that is the ultimate real point – a point that, in conformity with what Lacan says, can't be symbolized. Spinoza, for example, names an ultimate point that is the intellectual intuition of God, but he doesn't give any real intuition of it. The proof of this is that the best approximation of it is the beatitude felt in mathematics. But mathematical knowledge is knowledge of the second kind, not the third. As such, the intuition of the ultimate point remains elusive. As for Plato, he expressly declares, in the *Republic*, that he can only give an image of the Good, and nothing else.

The Immanence of Truths will partly be a tentative to delimit as much as possible this point, in the hope of reducing it as a point of ineffability. It will be a question of making it as minimally ineffable as possible, and, hence, as transmissible as possible. I don't know right now, for all that, how far I'll have to go in this direction.

– In this respect, you're not a Platonist: you want to transmit your ultimate intuition whereas Plato seems to give up on this.

– Plato starts from a philosophical experience, and the necessity to transmit this is, for him, external to the experience itself. That's why he maintains that philosophers have to be forced to become politicians and pedagogues. Once they're led to the Idea of the Good, they'll have a single idea, which is to stay there! This necessity to transmit, which originates outside of the experience of truth itself, is for Plato a social and political exigency. This experience has to be able to be shared on the level of society's overall organization. If you don't transmit it, you leave people under the influence of prevailing opinions. It's necessary, then, 'to corrupt' youth, in the sense of Socrates: i.e., to convey the means by which they can avoid being subjugated to prevailing opinions. I fully share this view of philosophy. And I'm very attached, as is well known, to its didactics.

The question of the nature of truth remains obscure in Plato. He didn't really say what truth is. Thus, is the Idea of the Good theological in nature? We know that there have been contradictory interpretations of Plato. Galileo and many others were able to consider him as the very example of scientific rationalism. Yet, the Neo-Platonists held him to be the very example of transcendent theology. These divergences are explained by the fact that Plato didn't say much concerning the truth to which he refers.

For me, truths exist; I describe them, and I've said and will say again explicitly – in *The Immanence of Truths* – how and why they exist. It's true that transmission is difficult in this instance. What has to be transmitted is that truths, qua bodies that exist,[2] are an exception from the rest. Plato himself, moreover, equally presents the Idea of the Good as exceptional. The Idea of the Good is not an Idea! It far exceeds the Idea in precedence and power, according to a much commented-upon passage of the *Republic*.[3] What could this possibly

---

[2] The original French reads '*Ce qu'il faut transmettre, c'est que les vérités, en tant qu'elles existent . . .*', which could have been translated simply as 'What has to be transmitted is that truths, *insofar as they exist . . .*', with the locution 'insofar as' having the same value here as it does, for example, in Aquinas' declaration in the *Summa Theologica*: 'For all existing things, insofar as they exist, are good, since the existence of a thing is itself a good.' That said, 'insofar as' can also suggest a conditional modality, which is what the more explicative formulation given here has sought to rule out. [Translator's note]

[3] The passage of *The Republic* Badiou is referring to in the text is 509b. [Translator's note]

be? Negative theology will say that it's God, and that of God nothing can be said. On the side of rationalism, there's the interpretation put forward by Monique Dixsaut and many others – myself included – that consists in showing that there is a principle of intelligibility that isn't reducible to the Idea itself. That the Idea is a principle of intelligibility exceeds, of course, the Idea.

Plato is a founding figure and extremely important for me, but it has to be acknowledged that he's evasive. There's an obliquity in his texts, which is facilitated, moreover, by the dialogue form since you never exactly know who is speaking and who speaks the truth. The dialogue flows like a stream; in the end, you've clearly grasped the problem but not the solution. You don't know exactly where Plato stands. It's somewhat of a contrived let-down. For example, Socrates' interlocutors in the *Republic* at one stage point out to him that it's high time he defined this Idea of the Good that he's been talking about for way too long already. We then see Socrates put on airs, and more or less say: 'you're asking far too much of me!'

This is not my style. I try, on the contrary, to say as much as I possibly can. I'm a more affirmative and less evasive Platonist than Plato. At least, I try! This is to do with the conception I have of philosophy as an exercise in transmitting something that you could make do with declaring impossible to transmit. In this sense, we're dealing with the impossible that is specific to philosophy; that is its goal, its end. I am, then, engaged in the battle against contemporary scepticism, cultural relativism and generalized rhetoric, just as Plato fought against the sophists. It's a matter for me of maintaining that truth is an exception but of not declaring it intransmissible for as much, since this would mean putting myself in a really weak position vis-à-vis the prevailing nihilism.

I nevertheless leave open the possibility that truth might, as seems to be case for Plato, be fairly difficult to transmit. In this respect, it's very interesting to note the educational curriculum set out in the *Republic* for the student of philosophy. This consists, in progressive order, of Arithmetic, Geometry, Geometry in space, Astronomy, and Dialectic. That said, in the passage on the dialectic, as anyone can see, there's nothing! All that is set down, then, is that learning philosophy is based on mathematics and astronomy, and thus explicitly referred to a scientific condition. Beyond this basis, 'dialectic' names something different – but what this is isn't any clearer than the Idea of the Good.[4]

– What do you think of Bergson's famous thesis that every philosopher finds in his or her consciousness an unseizable point: 'In this point is something simple, infinitely simple, so extraordinarily simple that the philosopher has never succeeded in saying it. And that is why he went on talking all his life.'[5]

– If in my philosophy I see a point of this type, it's the one that we've just outlined and identified, which involves, in fact, thinking through-and-through the subjectivization of truth – and not simply the existence of the truth process. This is what I name incorporation, grasped not in its objective logic but taken up this time from the point of view of the subject. The intuition of this incorporation is generally accompanied by a specific affect that is, no doubt, nothing other than this feeling of transmission's difficulty we've been speaking about.

---

[4] In the original French text, the letter 'i' of 'idée' (here: 'Idea') is left in small letters rather than being capitalized. This is a typographical error, as confirmed by the authors. [Translator's note]

[5] Henri Bergson, 'Philosophical intuition' [1911], in *The Creative Mind,* trans. M. L. Andison, Totowa, Littlefield, Adams and Co., 1965, p. 109. Reprinted in *Henri Bergson. Key Writings,* edited by Keith Ansell Pearson and John Mullarkey, London and New York, Continuum, 2002, p. 234

This problem is going to be the object of the work I'm planning to write and which we've just discussed.

I'd hesitate, however, to say that simplicity is the obstacle. This simplicity is obviously typical of Bergson's ontology, which is an ontology that's not mathematical but vitalist. The radical point of a vitalist ontology consists in placing oneself in the pure differential of movement or pure duration – which is precisely what constitutes the experience of absolute simplicity and, at the same time, the foundation of thought for Bergson. But when the ontology is mathematical, as in my case, one starts with an intrinsic complexity, a pure multiplicity that doesn't refer to any primordial simplicity other than the void. That nothing can be said, moreover, of the void is obvious.

In the end, I agree with Bergson that there is a primordial point of experience – a point that all philosophical teaching attempts to lead back to and to transmit. Yet, I think that the experience of this point is the concentrated experience of a complexity and not the experience of a simplicity. I'm pretty much in agreement with Spinoza when it comes down to it. The example Spinoza proposes of the third kind of knowledge, absolute and intuitive knowledge, is that of a mathematical proof that would be encapsulated in a point.[6] I'm happy with this. When you've truly understood a mathematical proof, you don't need to go through the stages any more: you've understood something that's concentrated in a point. That said, didactics

[6] In *Ethics*, part II, proposition XL, Scholium 2, Spinoza provides a mathematical example in which one is given three numbers and required to find the fourth number, which is to the third as the second is to the first. This could, Spinoza notes, be resolved in a non-intuitive, mediated or procedural way – e.g., by multiplying the second and the third numbers, and then dividing them by the first – but it could also be resolved intuitively, without any mediating process. [Translator's note]

is obliged to go through the stages again because this point has a complexity – a complexity that is hidden insofar as we're dealing with a point. It's not the same thing to have a contracted complexity and a pure simplicity as in Bergson.

– How is it possible to be both a Platonist and a materialist? According to the criteria of academic philosophy, this is a contradictory stance. Would this unexpected synthesis constitute your force?

– I'll start from something that I was particularly struck by. Althusser himself maintained, particularly forcefully, that philosophy's main contradiction was between materialism and idealism. That said, in order to follow through this thesis under the conditions of modern materialism, taking into account mathematics, modern science, and materialism's overall results, he found himself forced to introduce the notion of 'random materialism'. For a great number of reasons – of which the most spectacular is the development of quantum mechanics – the question of chance had, ineluctably, to be introduced into any form of contemporary materialism. In the thoroughly materialist perspective that is mine, the objective existence of multiplicities is bordered, if I can put it this way, by the possibility of randomness; by the possibility that something occurs that couldn't be foreseen or calculated, nor reincorporated on the basis of the existing state of things. There's something like a random absolute point – random in the sense that it defies being organized by that of which it's a product. I don't need anything else. And I don't depart from materialism, which is in no way intrinsically constrained to have an organic connection with determinism. Determinism was merely one possible conception of materialism.

Determinism is insufficient, as has been known since the very beginning of materialism since, as early as primitive atomism, the *clinamen*, that sudden deviation of atoms that is without rhyme or reason, introduces an event that is removed (*soustrait*) from any determination – as I've elaborated at length in *Theory of the Subject*. I especially admire the first – heroic and coherent – materialists, Democritus, Epicurus and Lucretius, who, in a world full of gods and superstitions, introduced the radical thesis that atoms and the void are all there is. They had, however, to face up to the fact that they couldn't deduce the event of the world from atoms and the void alone. A third term is needed, in the form of a pure chance. In the end, when I say that 'there are only bodies and languages, except that there are truths', I'm making an Epicurean gesture. I'm stating there is an exception. But this exception is itself based solely on the existence of the event. And the event is nothing other than the possibility of randomness in the structure of the world.

– For you, an event always belongs to a context. It necessarily emerges in a world. There isn't, then, an event of the world itself?

– There isn't any event of the world. There are events in the world. There are local breaks. But in any case, I don't at all think that I depart from materialism by introducing events. Some have judged that this constitutes a new dualism. People have said to me that my introducing exception means that what I'm doing is no longer materialism. Yet it so happens that the consequences of an exception are wholly situated in a world. There isn't a sensible level and an intelligible level, a level of the event and a level of the world that are distinct. I maintain, moreover, that we can interpret Plato in doing away with this duality of the sensible and the intelligible, which belongs rather to a vulgar Platonism. Admittedly, Plato often expresses himself in these terms, but we mustn't forget his evasive, wily side or his constant use of images.

To come back to the event, to the random, it's necessary to insist on the existence of a break. There is a before and an after. This break doesn't cause a transition from an inferior world to a superior world. We're still in the same world. Certainly, the consequences of the break have a status of exception in relation to that which doesn't depend on the break. But it's necessary to show that these consequences are organized in accordance with the general logic of the world itself. This is a demonstration, a labour, which I impose upon myself each time. My old-Marxist friends, like Daniel Bensaïd, who accuse me of introducing a miraculous element, are simply mechanical materialists – of the variety that Marx, already, and even Lucretius, crossed swords with.

Dialectic

– A question on the dialectic. The impression can be had that you started off from the dialectic in your philosophical youth but that this approach then faded away. Some would say, however, that this isn't the case and point to a dialectical logic that links together your three works *Theory of the Subject*, *Being and Event* and *Logics of Worlds*. What would you say about these divergences between people who comment on or interpret your work?

– I believe that it is, in fact, possible to consider my philosophical undertaking as a vast traversal of the dialectic, as my friend Bruno Bosteels maintains, in a sense perhaps different from mine. I've maintained, throughout, the idea that truths' ontological status is one of exception: exception of the generic in relation to that which is constructible, exception of objectifiable bodies in relation to ordinary bodies, and exception of my materialism in relation to a simplistic materialism for which there are only bodies and languages. Now, the category of exception is a dialectical category because the thinking of exception always takes place on two contradictory fronts. An exception must be thought as a negation because it is not reducible to what is ordinary, but it must also not be thought as a miracle. It, therefore, has to be thought as internal to the process of – non-miraculous – truth, but thought, nonetheless, as an exception.

This is perhaps what Lacan meant by 'extimate': both intimate and exterior to the intimate. Here, we're well and truly in the core of the dialectic. In Hegel, for example, the negation of a thing is immanent to this thing but, at the same time, it goes beyond this thing. The core of the dialectic is this status of negation as an operator that at once separates and includes. In this sense, I'd say that I'm constantly in the dialectic, especially in *Theory of the Subject*, which is a book that's still very bound to classical Marxism and its developments along Maoist lines.

– *Theory of the Subject* is truly an astonishing, baroque, book. Is it possible to say that it deals with the four conditions simultaneously?

– Yes, there isn't any general theory of the four conditions in this book, any more, for that matter, than there's a general theory of the event. The fundamental categories of *Being and Event* are only implicit, being that by means of which it would be possible to unify what remains somewhat fragmentary in *Theory of the Subject*. But it can be said that, from one end to the other of my philosophical undertaking, I pursue a meditation on negation. I seek simply to account for the possibility of change – how it's possible to go from a given regime of the laws of that which is to another such regime – by the mediation of the protocol of a truth and its subject. I am, therefore, in dialectical thought. But as my dialectical thought includes a figure of chance, it's non-deterministic. I would remind you that the Hegelian dialectic is relentlessly deterministic. In this respect, it's a big theory typical of the nineteenth century. It is the spectacle of the auto-development of the absolute in the immanent necessity of this development. I'm obviously very far from all that. This is why the relation I have to Hegel is both close and complicated. It shouldn't be forgotten that in my three major books, Hegel is an author that is discussed in great detail: in *Theory of the Subject*, concerning the dialectical process itself; in *Being and Event*, concerning the infinite; and in *Logics of Worlds*, concerning being-there, the categories of being-there. I've always had a close dialogue with Hegel then, but also with Marx, Lenin and the great dialectical revolutionaries, concerning the political condition. It's simply that, with the presence of a random element, I introduce the principle of a break that isn't exactly homogeneous to the standard principles of negation.

– Since we do need to conclude . . . , could you tell me how you'd define philosophy?

– Philosophy is that singular discipline of thought that has as its departure point the conviction that there are truths. From there, it is led towards an imperative, a vision of life. What is this vision? That which has value for human individuals, that which grants them a genuine life and orients their existence, is the participation within these truths. This presupposes the construction, which is highly complicated, of an apparatus by means of which truths can be discerned: an apparatus by means of which one can circulate among truths and render them compossible. And all this in terms of our contemporaneity.

Philosophy is this trajectory. It starts off from life, then, and ends up at life. What does the epoch in which we live give us? What is this epoch? What things have value therein? What things don't? Philosophy proposes a sorting procedure amid the confusion of experience, from which it draws an orientation. This elevation of confusion to orientation[7] is the philosophical operation par excellence and its specific didactics.

This presupposes a concept of truth. This 'truth' can very well receive another name. Thus, there's a whole part of Deleuze's work in which what we're calling here 'truth' is called 'sense'. I can identify, in any philosopher whatsoever, what I would, for my part, have called 'truth'. This can be named 'Good', 'spirit', active force', 'noumenon' . . . I choose 'truth' because I assume classicism.

A selection is, as a result, necessary, and for this you need a sorting machine, that is, a concept of truth. It's necessary to show that this truth really exists but that there aren't, for all that, miracles and there isn't any need to have transcendent frameworks. Some philosophers hold to these transcendent frameworks. This isn't my way. We come, then, to the simple question, the question posed at the start: what is it to live? What is an intense and dignified life that cannot be reduced to strict animal parameters?

– What, in your view, would the affect specific to philosophy be?

– I think that philosophy must include, both in its conception and in what it proposes, the conviction that the true life can be experimented with immanently. Something has to indicate this from within itself, not simply in the way of an external imperative, like a Kantian

---

[7] In the original French text, this phrase erroneously reads '*Cette élévation de la confusion à l'élévation*', with the word 'elevation' being repeated in the place of the word 'orientation'. [Translator's note]

imperative. This is a matter of an affect, which indicates, or signals, immanently that life is worthwhile living. There's a formula in Aristotle I like a lot and that I readily take up: 'Live as an immortal.' There are other names for this affect: 'beatitude' in Spinoza, 'overman' in Nietzsche. I believe that there is an affect of the true life. This affect doesn't have any sacrificial component. Nothing negative is required. There isn't, as in religions, any sacrifice that will be compensated for in the future and elsewhere. This affect is the affirmative feeling of a dilation of the individual once he or she co-belongs to the subject of a truth.

I've come to understand relatively recently Plato's incredible obstinacy to prove that the philosopher is happy. The philosopher is happier than all those – the rich, the sensualists and the tyrants – who are commonly believed to be happier than s/he is. Plato comes back to this over and over again. He proffers countless demonstrations of this point: only whosoever lives under the sign of the Idea is truly happy, and s/he is the happiest of all. What this means is fairly clear: the philosopher's own life is to be an experimentation of what the true life consists in.

Philosophy is, then, three things. It's a diagnosis of the epoch: what does the epoch propose? It's a construction, on the basis of this contemporary proposition, of a concept of truth. And, finally, it's an existential experience relative to the true life. The unity of the three is philosophy. But at a given moment, philosophy is *a* philosophy. When I've finished writing *The Immanence of Truths*, and have, thereby, assured the contemporary unity of the three components of any philosophy, I'll be able to say: philosophy is me.

6

A Short Introduction to Alain Badiou's Philosophy

Fabien Tarby

Who is Alain Badiou? An eternal Maoist? A terrorist of the intellect with perilously left-wing leanings? Unless he is the author who has fascinated specialists of contemporary philosophy for the last twenty years at least, and whose name is known in philosophical circles the whole world over, from Sydney to Buenos Aires. A terrorist undoubtedly, but of hermeticism this time; a man whose philosophical declarations happen to be laced with mathematical bombs.

We are immediately brought face to face here with this mysterious Alain Badiou, whose name functions at times as an extremist foil, while, at others, it is the (prestigious but worrying) marker of an abstract and complicated thought. His political positions are a thunderous perturbation in the overly serene skies of our televisual democracy's daily regime. His is the heresy of an engagement that would have committed the crime of not condemning the crimes of Mao. Nevertheless, no specialist denies the complexity, the originality and the creative force of his philosophical works.

Badiou's celebrity – whether justified or ambiguous – mustn't conceal the fact that he is a philosopher in the purest sense of the word. He is a philosopher in the same sense that Plato, or Spinoza, or Leibniz, is: by virtue of a will to truth that finds expression in a perfectively constructed and untiringly tested system. Is this sufficient to describe him also as a *classical* philosopher? Such a characterization may well need to await the sanction of centuries. It nonetheless remains the case that Badiou's philosophy displays obvious classical features.

A classical philosopher, a philosophical system

His thought aims at resolving the eternal problems posed by that strange and unsettling, but profoundly human, activity that is named 'philosophy'. The postmodern trend, of which Derrida is the best representative, deconstructed thought's basic coordinates by referring to the ambiguity of language. It cast suspicion on any clear and affirmative ambition. Plato had already had to combat the sophists and to recall that philosophers, unlike these verbal jousters, start not with the ambiguity of words but with things. Classical philosophers affirm; their task is not negation, deconstruction, or suspicion. It is completely possible to construct, against the spectres of relativism and scepticism, a rational and veridical discourse on the universe and the human condition. Truth exists, and philosophy is the expression of this existence. Philosophy has, moreover, always expressed this, in different configurations, and the great systems (Plato, Hegel) are the basis on which we can chart a history of truth. There is, in a classical philosopher's view, a history of truth, which is progressively elaborated in reference to problems and theses that are themselves eternal. A body of thought is classical when it participates in this history.

As a vast construction progressively setting out, in an ordered fashion, a body of ideas that were asserted from the beginning, Badiou's philosophy is well and truly systematic. Three great expositions mark its stages, namely: *Theory of the Subject* (1982), *Being and Event* (1988) and *Logics of Worlds* (2006). All three are heavily influenced by mathematical and logical forms. The study of mathematics and logic provides the surest of frameworks for exploring the eternal problems of philosophy. A philosopher armed in this manner is a formidable thinker since thought guided by deduction is naturally systematic. Mathematics and logic do not lie, nor do they, from the sharpened tip of their inquiry, obfuscate or defer the answer. On condition that you can endure them, all is clear and distinct.

This feature of Badiou's thought goes hand in hand with another: his fidelity to the figure of the dialectic. There is dialectic as soon as thought becomes aware that the category of negation is indispensable if it is to grasp the totality of things. This category takes the form of an exception for Badiou. There is, then, something that eludes mathematics and logic. There isn't a dictatorship of form. On the contrary: while form, logic and mathematics are, unquestionably, the order of things, human beings have the surprise of partially escaping this through an elevation to a different order, which is that of exception and transgression. Humanity and the *event* go together. *Being* – which is mathematizable and logical – enters into a dialectic relation with the *event* qua human exception; whence, *Being and Event*.

Classicism is not synonymous here with the rumination and repetition of age-old texts. To accede to it, you require a new vision of the perennial problems facing thought, a vision revisiting and reviving thought's oldest problems through the lenses of mathematism and the dialectic of being and event. Nor is systematization to be understood as a deadening enterprise, dictating the exclusion of everything that doesn't fit within its framework, while flattering itself on holding the answer to everything. For the event is surprise, upheaval,

indeterminacy. It is the core of human reality – a reality
it weaves with the four threads of politics, love, art and
science, which are equally four networks comprised of
surprises and creations, four paths of truth.

Badiou's work, which spans some forty odd years,
manifests a multiform vitality. It is composed of
extremely technical, philosophical texts, literary prose,
theatrical plays, and political and polemical books. Its
classical and systematic character goes hand in hand,
therefore, with an appetite for the contemporary world,
an extreme attention to the present time. The series of
texts published in *Polemics*, as well as books such as
The Meaning of Sarkozy,[1] show this: they deal with
political questions posed today, such as the veil and
secularism, France's relation with Germany, and Jean-
Marie Le Pen's making it to the second round of the
French presidential elections in 2002.[2]

Further yet, the thematic scope of the work ranges
from art to love, politics to science. These movements

---

[1] *Polemics*, trans. Steve Corcoran, London and New York, Verso,
2006; *The Meaning of Sarkozy*, trans. David Fernbach, London,
Verso, 2008. Both Badiou's book on Sarkozy and most of the texts
in *Polemics* were originally published in France in a series named
Circonstances ['Circumstances']. Tarby's reference to this series by
name in his text has not been retained here – having been replaced
by the relevant English-language references – but it should be noted
that the series' title obviously underlines the 'circumstantial' nature
of these texts bearing on contemporary issues. [Translator's note]
[2] Founder and president – until 2011 – of the far Right, extremist
party *Le Front National*, Le Pen caused a major upheaval in French
politics by polling more votes in the first round of the 2002 elections
than the main Left candidate, the socialist Lionel Jospin, who had
been expected to confront the incumbent president and leader of the
right-wing Republican party, Jacques Chirac, in the second round.
All parties, with the exception of the National Front and the Trotsky-
ist *Lutte ouvrière* – as well, of course, as Badiou's 'post-party organization' *L'Organisation politique* – called for opposing Le Pen, even
if it meant voting for Chirac. See on this, Badiou's 'Kosovo, 11
septembre, Chirac/Le Pen', in *Polemics*. [Translator's note]

manifest the conviction that the human being is situated at the core and the intersection of these possibilities. This is why politics, love, art and science are named 'conditions'. Conditions of the subject, on one hand, which is to say a space open to the most authentic and profoundly impelling possibilities offered by humanity. Conditions of philosophy, on the other, since philosophy, far from being the origin of everything, only exists at the confluence of these human activities. It interrogates that which constitutes *its* conditions and seeks to understand what is at stake in each of them, as well as in their co-existence.

The fundamental thesis on being

What is being? This is philosophy's most impenetrable enigma, its sphinx or phoenix. Philosophy begins with it, from the moment the first Greek thinkers set out in search of the principle of all things. For Pythagoras this principle was constituted by numbers. In a sense, Badiou takes up this intuition, the most ancient in Western philosophy. It constitutes a decisive element in the teaching of Plato, for whom mathematical forms belong to the 'intelligible' sphere, which is to say the highest and truest objects of thought: those that we attain when we've been capable of freeing ourselves from sensory and corporal dependencies.

It could be thought that mathematics lead, at best, to a Platonic type of idealism and, at worst, to numerological mysticisms and other Cabbalistic speculations. For Badiou, however, they function as a confirmation of *materialism*. Materialist philosophers refuse to give in to religious superstition and pose the existence of matter as the sole principle of being. This is a horizontal representation – a space of pure immanence that is also open – which refuses illusory, transcendent verticals, such as God or the soul. For Althusser, this amounted to 'no longer telling yourself stories'.[3] Auguste Comte, for his part, defined the materialist principle as a 'reduction of the higher to the lower.'[4] Thus, the mind is brain, and life's matter. Science is, as a result, the sole access to being. Epicurus developed the notion of atoms; La Mettrie, the thematic of the human being as merely a biological machine.[5]

Badiou belongs to this tradition. Yet he revamps it from start to finish. How? By organizing materialism on the basis of mathematical science. Materialism had previously been physical (Epicurus), biological (La Mettrie), or historical, dialectical and sociological (Marx), but it had never been connected to mathematics and logics on such a systematic scope. This constitutes the invention of a new form of materialism. The basis of matter is not revealed by biology or physics but by the mathematical and logical laws that organize its eternal composition.

Everything begins with this thesis: being is simply the infinity of multiplicities. It is not *a* being. To speak of being in the singular, as language irresistibly invites us to do, mustn't make us fantasize about some sort of unity of being: there are only multiplicities that are infinitely decomposable into new multiplicities. Nowhere

---

[3] In his later writings Althusser undertook a fresh reading of atomism, which he summed up in the principle that one should not tell oneself stories. See *Philosophy of the Encounter: Later Writings, 1978-87*, trans. G.M. Goshgarian, London, Verso, 2006. [Translator's note]

[4] See Comte, A., *A Discourse on the Positive Spirit* [*Discours sur l'esprit positif*, 1844], § 771, in which Comte maintains that 'materialism explains the higher in terms of the lower.' [Translator's note]

[5] The reference here is to Julien Offray de La Mettrie's *L'Homme machine*, published in 1748 and variously translated into English as *Man a Machine* or *Machine Man*. Rejecting the Cartesian dualism of mind and body, La Mettrie proposes an extensive description of the 'several springs which move the human machine'. [Translator's note]

is there any endpoint, either above or below: there is neither an initial One, nor an ultimate atom. Badiou was to have the fundamental and primary insight that mathematics is alone capable of describing this type of infinitely decomposable multiplicities. Set theory, as conceived by Georg Cantor and axiomatized by Ernst Zermelo and Abraham Fraenkel, is basically nothing other than a theory of multiplicities implying the existence of an *empty set*.

This theory is neither particular nor regional. It is the very theory of mathematics, its eternal basis. Numbers, functions, points, and arithmetical relations are, in fact, all derived from sets. Everything that is conceivable is made up of sets and elements, and these sets and elements are themselves compositions and decompositions without end. In short, infinity and multiplicities are the legitimate basis of everything there is. As a result, mathematics is alone capable of pronouncing on being: infinitely decomposable multiplicities can lead only to the void. Or, put another way, multiplicities consist uniquely of the void.

There is, then, no mystery of being. Certainly, human beings look for the secret of being; they generally seek to interpret the world and to discover the essence or meaning of things. They believe they find something 'significant' in things. But things don't have any meaning in themselves. They are infinitely decomposable, and that's all. This is where Badiou diverges absolutely from Heidegger, who is tirelessly in quest of a 'meaning of being'. But since there is no meaning, Heidegger's philosophy gradually, and inevitably, took a poetic form. Where we end up at, if we are set on speaking of the mystery of being, is merely its absence of meaning, which is to say its *void*. Heidegger spoke of *Being*, conferring to this a majesty, whereas he should have more humbly stated that there is simply being: multiplicities that extend to infinities and whose sole endpoint is the meaningless void.

There are two errors concerning the infinity of being, this infinite multiplicity: the first is the religious interpretation, which consists in conceiving the Infinite as a God. Yet nothing is more banal, in fact, than the infinite, which, weaving together all things, makes the world an endless composition and decomposition. The second error consists in believing that the infinite is a joyful and unfathomable chaos. This is Deleuze's error. Deleuze remains a romantic of the infinite, or a sorcerer's apprentice: he would like the world to be like literary magic or, in other words, an all-encompassing, gigantic vortex, whereas it is, on the contrary, clearly made up of laws and constancies. The infinite consists in strict rules and mathematics.

These are the main contributions of *Being and Event*. *Logics of Worlds* then goes on to show that the way things appear depends upon a *logic*. How is it that things seem to us to be unified and formed into aggregates, all while being able to be known from a variety or a succession of different perspectives? I approach a familiar object and observe it from different angles, both close-up and from afar: I can say that it belongs to my office and my apartment, but also that it belongs to this city, to this solar system.

Idealist philosophies assume that there is a divine order in the world, or ground this order on a demiurgic capacity of human thought, such that it is consciousness or the mind that would give form to the world. This is what Kant does, as well as Husserl. For Badiou, phenomena, which is to say things such as they appear, neither express a divine order nor depend upon an ordering consciousness. Multiplicities are combined on different levels, according to intensities of appearance that vary. Perceiving things as small or large is relative since it depends on the point of view we have on things. Our vision itself depends on these logical rules. 'Worlds' are thereby constituted that set down different regimes. In strict conformity with the logic called 'the logic of categories', this pencil and this piece of paper on this desk can be shown to have a large intensity in the world that is this room but a zero intensity in the world of a Beijing worker. Ultimately, there are only worlds, to infinity; the relativity of these worlds is coherent and deducible. Infinity is not chaotic but ordered. Order is not divine or spiritual, but logical. And it would be illusory to believe that a unified Universe synthesizes this irreducible plurality.

From *Being and Event* to *Logics of Worlds* some thousand-odd pages develop, therefore, an integrally rational and materialist conception of the universe. Everything is mathematizable; everything is logical. The conclusions that are drawn from this are as radical as they are classical: this mathematics and this logic prove the infinity of being. In the same way, Spinoza and Leibniz were to find support in mathematics for their intuition of an infinite world. Yet neither of them forgoes a God, who would function as the principle of this infinite – be this a substantial principle, as in Spinoza's case, or a regulatory one, as for Leibniz. This principle is done away with in Badiou's materialism. Far from being signs of a divine order, the mathematics of being and the logic of appearing are, as a result, the very implementation of atheism.

Everything consists of structures alone . . .

What happens once we've understood that the universe is this infinite machinery? It's possible for nothing to happen – everything, always, being reduced to the rules by which such a machinery functions. This is something to wonder at: all things are intertwined, from the infinitely small to the infinitely large, and not only in space but logically and mathematically. The human outlook can, in fact, limit itself to the discovery of this sort of inhumanity where human beings exist, take up a place, and live. Such an outlook would have, at least, grasped the true sense of materialist wisdom and dispelled numerous persistent and infantile illusions regarding God or the absolute Meaning of life. All of which isn't nothing . . . but which isn't all. Badiou is not a nihilist who is satisfied to say that there is no underlying meaning to the universe, as does a whole tradition that goes from Gorgias to Clément Rosset, via Schopenhauer. Such defeatism isn't at all Badiou's cup of tea. Certainly, structures are inhuman by virtue of being superhuman or infinite, but they are, nonetheless, *only* structures, however ineluctable and all-pervasive they may be.

Mathematical and logical structures say to human beings: 'Whoever you may be, whatever you may do, you are inside; you are in the immanence of a situation or a world that is far greater than you. You are inside, you are included. You are not God, and there isn't, moreover, any God.' This is to be taken for granted. Neither our thought nor our acts will ever succeed in destroying or transforming the order of the mathematical and physical materiality that encircles us from birth to death. We will always be *within*, determined as we are by that which, in us, can be called the 'human animal': that being that is subjected to the laws of things, which are as much mathematical, physical and biological laws as psychical ones.

Yet, ending up at nihilism, at impotence, and concluding that human existence or the human condition is absurd, is the step that we are refusing to take here. It's necessary to be a strict materialist, a philosopher who thinks that we are surrounded by materiality, without any meaning other than the implacable and infinite meaning yielded by mathematics and logic. God – this Father Christmas for adults – is absent. This is understood. For all that, however, to restrict ourselves to structures' inhuman inflexibility – and 'inhuman' simply because it's superhuman – is to fail to see what we are capable of. Capable of, by chance perhaps, but this chance changes just about everything.

While idealist philosophers were venerating their totems, materialist philosophers had to confront the question of whether there wasn't, all in all, anything other to human beings than their animality. The transcendence or verticality of idealists – going all the way to the soul or God – is no doubt illusory. Yet, can materialists, on their side, remain in a definitive and absolute horizontality, where it would suffice to say that human beings are human animals? Can our strange reality – the fact of being 'me', being 'you' – be reduced to instinctive animality? Were this the case we would neither write nor read, for we wouldn't be traversed by what Lacan calls the symbolic and which changes our fundamental relationship to a real, which, for this reason, is no longer immediate. The consciousness of an individual murmuring, with stupefaction, that s/he is going to die, testifies to this.

It's a matter of knowing what materialism will make of this irreducibly human perspective. There has never, in fact, been a materialism capable of maintaining a horizontal purity. There has always been some sort of supplement or parenthetical clause. There was a force of mind, albeit atomic, for Epicurus, which was the means by which one could understand reality and choose the good life; there was a liberating laughter and irony for La Mettrie; while, for Marx, there was a refusal of immediate reality, on the one side, and hope, in the form of communism, on the other. Materialism's impossibility to completely reduce human beings to matter can give us a lot to mull over. In truth, materialism is, *first*, this recovered lucidity concerning the nature of the real and the inexistence of God, which *then* liberates. Its lesson is without illusion: give up enigmas, realities are rude. Yet, its perspective is neither one of submission nor of acceptance. There is, by chance, in human beings, something that eludes the infinite platitude of being. There is, in human beings, something else.

Badiou is faithful to this profound insight of a materialism that always exceeds itself in its human component. He extends this insight, amplifies it and raises it to a level that is, strictly speaking, unsupportable. Indeed, his version of materialism's going beyond itself is as dazzling as his materialism of structures is strict, mathematical and logical. Badiou's originality is to carry the two planes of materialism to their most intense expression: on the one hand, there is no concession whatsoever on the simultaneously rational and meaningless nature of the real, which requires we conceive this real as absolutely mathematical; but, on the other, there is the acute awareness that, with human beings, *something happens*, for them and by them. This something exceeds the structures, at least at the point of its existence.

This is what the *event* is. Something happens, which is precisely not a thing: it is not an element or a set of elements in the structure that is present – which Badiou likes to call the *situation*. Something is capable of partially disrupting the situation. To the extent that the latter is a given, determined and organized, structure, the event is the sudden irruption within this scene of a set of things, of elements, that were neither given nor determined. If we follow this thought through to the end, it can be said that the event is the occurrence or the flash, the dazzling revelation or an instant, of the void subjacent to the situation, buried in the structures.

It has to be pointed out here that the structure generally deprives the event of existence. It represses it. When an event occurs, it can, then, be compared to a surprising resurfacing of elements that were, until then, not presented in this situation. This surprising emergence of the underlying void causes hitherto unknown elements to be presented suddenly in the situation. On the eve of a revolution, everything can seem in order (this is the structure), yet, at dawn, suddenly, something happens that the structure hadn't anticipated: people ready for anything, rifles slung over their shoulders, their heads full of ideas. This event doesn't, for all that, come out of nowhere. Its resources lay dormant in the depths. This force is suddenly revealed, and while it gives the structure the impression of a void that has come to the surface, it is also, and above all, the upheaval of the situation.

Of truth and the incredible purview of a fidelity

The concept of *fidelity* is immensely important. It designates the act by which we commit ourselves to the disruptive consequences of an event. Human beings assume the event and find themselves changed because of it. They become *subjects* of the event. Being faithful to the event consists in seizing this chance. It consists in living by virtue of the event and for the event. It consists in no longer being merely the animal entrusted, up to its dying day, to meaningless being; it consists in creative humanity.

For this, it's necessary to name the event, to recognize its trace and to become '*incorporated*' within it. It is always possible to deny the event, in the manner of the *subject* that Badiou qualifies as *reactive*. Such a subject buries the event in the being of things – which is easy to do, given the unfailing neutrality of being. In 1871, just at the time when the last Communards were being executed, the headlines of one Paris newspaper, *Le Siècle*, read 'The Social Crisis is being resolved.' Nothing then had happened. 'Nothing took place . . . but the place', as Badiou likes to say, following Mallarmé. So we find, today, negationists of the event May '68, who make it out to be a thing of the past or a simple senseless flurry of unrest, whereas there are others who are faithful to this event and who perpetuate its sense.

We can then deny the event, just as we can also be completely mistaken about its signification by failing to grasp its two most human characteristics. First, the event situated, is always relative to a situation; it cannot change everything, it can simply disrupt local situations. We don't 'break History into two', as Nietzsche hoped; we transform situations from inside, which isn't nothing, and which saves us from a misguided nihilism or the out-and-out despair of powerlessness. Second, the human dimension of the event is lost if we imagine that it conveys a final, determined and substantial Truth.

The fact is that no given end whatsoever can be assigned to the trajectory that the event opens up to the subject. Its meaning remains open and, because of this, living. Believing that truth is precisely and uniquely This or That is to make the event a simulacrum. That which is essential is lost sight of, namely that the truth of an event remains indiscernible or, as Badiou likes to say, 'generic': the existence of this truth modifies our knowledge – which henceforth searches for it – but it is not itself something that can be known in a perfectly determined way. There is, as a result, no end to the search, which only puts forward hypotheses concerning truth. Truth is, in this respect, similar to what are named *generic* sets, which have been shown to exist by the mathematician Paul Cohen even though their composition is unknown.

Everyone is well aware that love consists in a trajectory, a construction, or a voyage undertaken together within life situations and countless structures, such as families, living spaces, friends and professions. But who could say in what exactly the truth of a love consists? The path is undetermined and open: it makes its way, passing through incidents and stages, without either of the two lovers being in complete possession of its meaning. Nor does either of them know what will come of it. You can say, 'I love you' and be faithful to this declaration, but you cannot say what this love is that makes us live things and situations together as 'two', and which has its source in the mystery of sexual difference. Love is much more a matter of acts than it is of representations. Even the birth of a child isn't, for love, a point of arrival but a new situation to share. Truth constantly constructs itself here in what can be called a 'truth procedure'. It cannot be defined or grasped objectively; yet, nor is it nothing: it acts and produces itself as a procedure.

Truth is, then, concrete: it is not a simple mental representation; it is what we make of our love. That a truth is indiscernible or generic not only doesn't take anything away from the value of the trajectory that is integrated within it, but is, indeed, what makes it possible for a subject to exist. When you believe, on the contrary, that you possess the truth of love, when you think that it is definitively This or That, then it is, in fact, lost.

Similarly, there is nothing more disastrous in politics than believing in a form of fullness that you proclaim to the detriment of *Universality*. Universality has a specific sense here. It doesn't signify an order of thought that ignores singularities but a wisdom of the indiscernible or the *generic* – in the sense we've just indicated. Whoever comes to think that that which is common to everyone isn't marked by singularities or by communities that differ – without, for all that, denying these singularities and their irreducible character – finds themselves incorporated within this universal. On the contrary, the 'obscure subject' refuses this universality that is open to all, beyond secondary or communitarian distinctions. This subject identifies truth with an ideology or a religion, which is to say a pseudo-knowledge taking the place of a living, undefined truth.

Living as a subject or happiness in the Idea

Alain Badiou is a thinker of the Idea. You might say that every philosopher is supposed, by definition, to have ideas. The fact remains that you have to know what 'having an Idea' actually means. Why, for example, is it necessary here to have a capital 'I'?

It isn't natural for human beings to refer to an Idea. Everything depends, first of all, on what is meant by 'human beings'. The 'human' can be reduced to the 'human animal' when it's a matter simply of processes that take place according to the natural laws of a body and a mind. The body seeks satisfaction; thought appropriates things egotistically, without going any further than superficial or routine reflections. How powerful this part of our being is, is something known to all of us. And we can easily lose that which is essential therein. There's no Idea in this case; simply an apathetic life. So-and-so mechanically kisses his wife, whom he basically doesn't love any more than his apartment. Someone else declares that 'we aren't governed all that badly, considering the overall situation and that you can't change the fact that there will always be people who are poor while others are rich'. Or, they may think about getting rich themselves: 'I don't give a damn about what happens when I'm gone ...' A third individual is happy to have simply an immediate or imaginary relation to the real, venturing out in the world guided merely by her instincts. A fourth, finally, doesn't see that a work of art could, in any way, be moving or the source of some kind of revelation, or simply believes that art has never been anything other than a sort of nursery rhyme.

The Idea is the possibility for every individual to bring out the best and the most elevated in themselves, and even, despite death, to attain to that which, in all of us, is immortal. Ideas are not, in other words, simple mental representations that are more or less illusory, or purely epiphenomena of the brain. There is a grandeur and dignity to the Idea. Elevating oneself to Ideas is a mode of being and living that human beings can make their own, and thereby realize that life is worthwhile being experienced to the full, and that a part – the most precious part – of themselves depends on this. This quintessence of what it is to be human, which isn't given naturally, is what Badiou names a *Subject*. As is clear, the Subject is not solely or essentially a consciousness, as it is for Descartes, nor is it that centre that is named 'I' or 'me', which organizes or formats the experience of the world – as is the case for Kant or Husserl.

This way of defining the Subject that can emerge within the human animal – potentially in spite of itself – doesn't split the world in two, in such a way that there would be exceptional individuals, on the one side, and human animals, on the other. The two tendencies exist in each of us: the ponderousness of the human animal that is satisfied with what there is, and the possible grace of the subject that opens itself up to *something else*, to the Idea.[6] We are permanently caught in this body and this mind that are ours, and yet we are, at the same time, disposed towards the best, but also the most exigent – to Ideas. No one is an exception to this; everyone lugs their existence from one to the other, from the human animal to the subject that is possible. Each human being is potentially a subject. As a result, the fundamental criticism that Badiou addresses to our time is that it has forgotten the Subject that is virtually

---

[6] The French word that has been translated here as 'ponderousness' is *pesanteur*, which, when coupled with *grâce* ('grace') immediately brings to mind the title of Simone Weil's *La Pesanteur et la grâce*, which has been translated into English as *Gravity and Grace*. The term 'gravity' doesn't immediately convey the sense desired by Tarby here; whence our choice of the term 'ponderousness'. [Translator's note]

present in the human animal. Constructing the Subject is an exigency. It's only too easy for us to forget or deny the Subject within ourselves; the social environment in which the animal is plunged day-in, day-out, contributes to this.

In the end, 'to live as a Subject', to live for the Idea, is a source of happiness, of felicity. Yet, we still have to be able to reach this possibility. We have to be able to encounter it, and sustain it with endurance – which requires all the more courage, or fidelity, to the extent that the things of the world will always threaten to extinguish the joy that we feel. There are a great many obstacles on the path rendering justice to that of which humanity is capable.

Our present time, for example, promotes a politics without any surprises. Vote for the Left or for the Right, vote and, then, just let politicians do as they choose. And all the while, the inequality between people is only equalled by the tranquil cynicism of capitalism. 'You have to accept the world as it is' – such is the endless refrain of the human animal. The latter adapts to this world, or appropriates it. The atmosphere of our time is permeated by an opiate propaganda. We have mass entertainment rather than the dazzling inscription of art in us, while the science that is promoted is showy and superficial, rather than having a real exigency. Likewise, we settle for a love that has become conventional, a single status that is egotistical or melancholic, or a hedonistic equivalence between desiring and loving. Is it though really a matter of love, if love is no different from satisfying our needs or walking in the street? If voting is no different from buying or consuming, is it really a political engagement?

Not that Badiou wants to condemn us to a painful exigency. When the subject lives in us, it is aware of the happiness of being incorporated, or of being faithful, to an Idea. It's better to fight for equality – that political Idea – than to accept the factual and structural inequality of the world; it's better to live for love, in the midst of tempests, banalities, and, no doubt, flying crockery, than for desire's banal injunction 'Enjoy!', which, as everyone, in fact, knows, is an injunction all in all insufficient or neurotic. To live for knowledge of the real, even though it may be hard to attain and will require my patience, but whose intuitive fruit I can already taste; to live for new knowledge, rather than for the smoke and mirrors of astrology, media stories or other such gibberish. To live for the joyful comprehension of the way in which a work of art transfixes me, rather than for mass-produced, non-stop entertainment.

It's impossible to understand what *incorporation* to the Idea means unless we abandon all conceptions of the psychological subject, all conceptions of what we think we are fundamentally, namely a 'self'. Subject and consciousness are not the same. A consciousness can be blind to the event, to its truth, to the Idea, and simply illuminate animal life. A subject must, of course, be conscious, for it wouldn't otherwise be capable of recognizing the event or its enduring trace, and of becoming faithful or incorporated to it. But being conscious isn't enough to elevate ourselves to the level of the subject. Likewise, we must, by the decisions we make, reaffirm this fidelity, and hold fast to the decisions made as the basis for continuing in the name of the event.

There is, then, in each individual who becomes a subject, an act of conscious recognition. Yet, we'd understand precious little about the subject were we to reduce it to the feeling or consciousness we have of being a person or a singular being: John, Alan, Isabel, Fabian . . . To become incorporated within an event precisely entails becoming dis-incorporated from our ego, from our own little selves – and, sometimes, even from our very body. There's no way, for instance, that a political body could be mine, any more than the Idea of equality has anything to do with the selfish thought of my own interests. A political body is common to the activists who share the same desire for equality. It is the multiplicity of thoughts and corporeal actions, demonstrations and slogans, that is oriented and relatively unified by this Idea, and within which 'I' simply become incorporated, participating thereby within the collective subject of politics. Only by going beyond yourself in this way, can you heed the event and become faithful to it. The subject is not the individual. It is the individual who becomes a subject by going beyond his or her affective and intellectual ego.

The four conditions

I can be literally carried away by a work of art, which jolts me out of the material routines making up my little world. Thanks to this work, a nascent form suddenly comes to light in what I had previously considered as completely formless. An impossible form becomes real. I can give myself up to this impossible that has become the artwork, just as I can resist it by refusing the truth it conveys in its guise of an event.

Let us listen to Schoenberg, for instance. The human animal would merely say that this music is 'boring' or 'disharmonious' – in the same way that romanticism was scandalous in the eyes of classicists – without penetrating its truth. This music, however, not only invents a new conception of scale but also allows us to grasp that the traditional scale is only one possibility among others. It conveys the infinite to human beings.

The affects of the human animal, who feels bored, or uneasy, or exasperated, before a work of art, are then obstacles to the artistic experience. They are also obstacles to our becoming a subject. The animal affects repel the happy affects that are those of the subject. For it so happens that, when we become faithful to the experience of a truth and we remain guided by the Idea, we feel thoroughly happy as a result. Nonetheless, this doesn't happen straightway, insofar as the duality of the animal and the subject remains a given.

Similarly, politics demands that we know how to become depersonalized and leave our natural baseness to one side, in order to become a subject. Nothing is more demanding. To take heed of the universal, to orient our own being (as well as everything in our personal situation that we can) towards this always undefined truth: this is what fighting for the Idea of equality entails. Fascisms and nationalisms deny this justice without limits; they have no conception of the universal, as a state without exception or hierarchy between individuals. The 'homeland' or 'national preference' are its negations. The 'communist hypothesis' proposes to humanity, on the contrary, the universal and equality. This hypothesis must not be judged on the basis of communist revolutions and dictatorships; identifying the truth that it conveys with the failures of history is too easy, and lets capitalism get away with its cynical dimension. Badiou speaks at times of a *generic communism* in order to underline that the Idea doesn't express the toxic history of the word 'communism'.

Those who identify the so-called extremes of communism and Nazism are, then, completely and utterly mistaken on the philosophical signification of communism. Communism is an admissible name for the sole political truth, which is the equality of all, without restriction. The Idea of communism has as its horizon the truth of politics, even should this truth need to be continually taken up again, insofar as there is neither an end nor a limit to it. This suffices to distinguish it from the dictatorial forms of state communism in the twentieth century. Capitalism, for its part, is the rapacious voracity of structures that are conceived and consented to on the basis of the model of the animal in human beings, or the human animal. Nations are themselves comparable to individual bodies, insofar as, like the latter, they are undeniable as natural realities or present structures; but they are not *truths*.

As for love, this is an experience of the Two. It is as Two that we live the experience of a faithful incorporation within the Idea. Through the event of the encounter and the fidelity then forged, together we make two whereas previously we were alone. Who is unaware that selfish desire is not yet love? Who fails to see that it's necessary to become other than oneself in order to love? There is here, contrary to the law of desire per se, the exigency of a depersonalization of egoism in the name of the Idea – the Idea of living from now on as two, of sharing a situation from two points of view. The subject of love is not, then, *he* or *she*, but that which in the *we* exceeds, and nonetheless coordinates, the one and the other, without there ever being a fusion, other than illusory. In love, one links oneself with another in order to form a subject with him or her.

Truth is experimented with, finally, in the condition that is science through a process similar to those observed in love, the work of art, and politics: namely, an asceticism by means of which our base nature is depersonalized. It's necessary to renounce our banal subjectivity, opinions and prejudices in order to attain objectivity. In this case, 'objectivity' is the name that can be given to a set of structures that convey what can be stated of the world and do so without any reference whatsoever to the singularity of individual points of view. Understanding numbers and counting, for example, have nothing to do with feelings or personal preferences.

Scientific knowledge can be considered, in the same way as art for example, to elaborate forms: namely, statements, theories, and protocols. These forms capture elements of experience, insights into the world, and characteristics of truths. They also let many other elements, etcetera, escape them. However, an event can suddenly take place – an experimental discovery, for example, or a brilliant theoretical synthesis connecting facts or theories that had, up to then, stood on their own. Every aspect of the relation between what was captured by the form and what still awaited capture is, as a result, transformed.

This, then, is an event in the order of science. Form conquers new territories, with this innovation radically changing certain aspects of knowledge that are reorganized in a new framework which encompasses them or gives them a different sense. So it was that Cantor's set theory profoundly modified the concepts of number and point in mathematics. These both became particular cases in a theory that is more general than arithmetics or Euclidean geometry.

Similarly, quantum physics transformed the deterministic conceptions that had seemed natural and absolutely specific to scientific knowledge. Theoretical formulae and mathematical calculations were henceforth to take account of the radical innovation represented by the indeterminacy of physical phenomena at an atomic scale. On this scale, everything is radically changed: causal relations, the determination of a property, the individuality of a particle of matter . . . What this entails is, indeed, a new relation between that which had been captured in the old formulae of classical determinism and that which remained dormant in mathematics. Scientific knowledge found itself enriched by the very thing – undetermined physical phenomena – that constituted an exception to it.

Yet, the power of an event to radically modify forms that had seemed self-evident is, doubtlessly, best shown by Einstein's theories of general and special relativity. Just as Schoenberg transformed musical forms that had seemed immutable, so Einstein overturned the all-too-human, all-too-empirical representations of space and time as well of these forms' relation.

The last word goes to ethics

We sometimes believe that truth is something that can be taken hold of, as though it were a form of knowledge that can be possessed; or we believe in the event as in a unique, definitive and total Revolution. This is what gives rise to fascist or nationalist, non-egalitarian political notions, jealous or selfish fusion in love, the refusal of artistic experimentations, and obscurantism in science. But human beings do not possess truths; the creative, infinite virtuality of truths is something they must, on the contrary, content themselves with receiving.

Being faithful to the event, which is the means by which we become a subject of truth, isn't always easy. Sooner or later, there will be political obstacles, domestic scenes or an indifference to the other, artistic discouragement, or scientific impasses. Yet, the *affects* of enthusiasm, happiness, pleasure and joy will enable me to overcome these difficulties – on condition that I continue to pursue the course of fidelity and incorporation. This is what *ethics* is. It isn't a body of predetermined moral rules. It consists in carrying on, in continuing on the path opened up, for me, by an authentic event.

Ethics also consists, then, in human beings' acknowledging the event's existence: in their believing in the event, believing that something can occur that changes what is given, or things as they are, in a real way and not simply seemingly, as when we mechanically zap from one TV programme to another. Who could not want the event, the Idea, truth, and the paradoxical, yet total, happiness of becoming incorporated therein?

A strict mathematics of being; but also a thought of the Idea, which is force and joy: Badiou is the name, in the history of philosophy, of a new synthesis between the rigorous lucidity of materialism and the invincible hope of idealism.